Greg Clydesdale lectures in the Department of Business Management at Lincoln University, Christchurch, New Zealand. He is the author of three books: *Entrepreneurial Opportunity*, *Human Nature*, and *Waves of Prosperity*. His articles have been published in a wide range of academic journals such as *Prometheus*, *Creativity Research Journal*, *Quarterly Journal of Austrian Economics* and *Entrepreneurship and Regional Development*.

ALSO AVAILABLE

Waves of Prosperity
Greg Clydesdale

Mr China
Tim Clissold

Chinese Rules: Five Timeless Lessons for Succeeding in China
Tim Clissold

The Art of War
Sun Tzu

*Chinese Whispers: Why Everything
You've Heard About China is Wrong*
Ben Chu

The Art of Business

GREG CLYDESDALE

ROBINSON

ROBINSON

First published in Great Britain in 2017 by Robinson

1 3 5 7 9 10 8 6 4 2

Copyright © Greg Clydesdale, 2017

A CIP catalogue record for this book
is available from the British Library.

'Qingming Shang Tu'or 'Along the River During the Qingming Festival' (detail),
Zhang Zeduan (1085–1145) original scroll painting dating from the Northern
Song Dynasty (960–1127) / Pictures from History / Bridgeman Images

ISBN: 978-1-47213-975-7

Typeset in Scala by Hewer Text UK Ltd, Edinburgh
Printed and bound in Great Britain by CPI Group (UK), Croydon CRO 4YY

Papers used by Robinson are from well-managed
forests and other responsible sources.

MIX
Paper from
responsible sources
FSC® C104740

Robinson
An imprint of
Little, Brown Book Group
Carmelite House
50 Victoria Embankment
London EC4Y 0DZ

An Hachette UK Company
www.hachette.co.uk

www.littlebrown.co.uk

Contents

Chinese Imperial Dynasties

Xia (c.2200 to 1600 BC)

Shang (c.1600 to 1045 BC)

Zhou (1045 to 256 BC)

    Spring and Autumn Period (722 to 476 BC)

    Warring States (475 to 221 BC)

Qin (221 to 206 BC)

Han (206 BC to AD 220)

Six Dynasties (AD c.220 to 581)

Sui (AD 581 to 618)

Tang (AD 618 to 907)

Five Dynasties (AD 907 to 960)

Song Dynasty

    Northern Song (AD 960 to 1127)

    Southern Song (AD 1127 to 1279)

Yuan (AD 1279 to 1368)

Ming (AD 1368 to 1644)

Qing (AD 1644 to 1911)

CHAPTER 1

The Art of Business

....

China is on track to become the world's biggest economy. By one measure, price purchasing parity, it is already the biggest in the world. This will not be the first time that China has been number one. In fact, for most of the past thousand years, it has been the largest market economy in the world. If in the year AD 1300, *Forbes* magazine had released a rich list, it would have been dominated by Chinese men. It was only in the eighteenth century that the West began to overtake China on the basis of innovations in trade, commerce and production.

Travellers to China consistently commented on the wealth of the country and level of commercial activity. This included Marco Polo who came from Europe's richest city, Venice, and the Moroccan traveller Ibn Battuta, who arrived not long after Marco Polo. Ibn Battuta was emphatic when he said 'there is no people in the world wealthier than the Chinese'[1]. Yet, people in the West know very little about Chinese business. For example, when Westerners look to Chinese history to enhance management practice, their most frequent reference is Sun Tzu's *The Art of War*; however, that book has nothing to do with business. It is, as its title suggests, about war.

Many academics have argued that this Chinese book on war provides ideal training for business. After all, war and business both involve confrontation and the need for positioning against a competitor. They both rely on organisation and management skills, and they both require the mobilisation of resources in pursuit of a strategy. However, there are substantial differences between war and business.

While both war and business involve strategy, business places prime importance on the customer. Military strategy, by contrast, shows no consideration for the customer (unless they are mercenaries). Strategy without consideration of the client has no role in business. Secondly, war and business may both involve competition but the nature of that competition is very different. In war, an army is juxtaposed against one enemy or an alliance. By contrast, businesses may face several competitors, each with its own agenda. The number of competitors has important implications when developing positioning strategies.

Perhaps the biggest difference comes from the function of military and business organisations. Businesses function to create and distribute value to customers. War, by contrast, does not have a purpose of providing value. In fact, it commonly destroys products and services that people value. The human values needed to conduct business are very different to those in war. Market economies are built on relationships where trust can be developed between businesses, clients and suppliers. This trust encourages them to spend and invest. By contrast, war places a priority on deception, a factor Sun Tzu stressed by saying, 'All warfare is based on deception.'[2]

Unsurprisingly, when writing this book, I found no evidence that *The Art of War* ever inspired Chinese business or management practice in the past. If Westerners have been reading Sun Tzu's book to understand Chinese business, they have been given a false impression. To gain a better idea of the influences on Chinese business, we need to look at the works that have shaped the activities of Chinese businessmen. Businessmen, wherever they live, must adapt to the environment in which they engage. In which case, it is important to understand the influences that have shaped the culture and environment in which Chinese businessmen act.

Around the same time that Sun Tzu wrote his famous work, a number of books appeared that had a much stronger influence on Chinese business. These influential books appeared in the late Spring and Autumn (722–476 BC) and Warring States (475–221 BC) periods. This was a time when philosophers across the Eurasian continent were coming to terms with issues of relevance to management; in particular, what is human nature and how is it best governed? In China, these issues were discussed by a number of philosophers from whom appeared three dominant schools of thought. These are Legalism, Taoism and Confucianism.

The school of Taoism is associated with a philosopher named Laozi or Lao Tzu, which can be translated as 'old master'. Lao Tzu is the author of the book *Tao Te Ching*. Written around the sixth century BC, this argues that there is a proper way to go in life. If we follow the 'Tao' which means the 'way' or the 'path', all will be in harmony. Taoism placed an emphasis on naturalness, simplicity and spontaneity.

If a leader followed the Tao, they would be in accord with nature and everything would work out – there would be no need for rules, regulations and prohibitions – but leaders do not follow the Tao and, consequently, people suffer. Taoists were against government intervention in society. This can be seen in one of the most famous quotations on Chinese leadership:

> *The best leaders are those their people hardly know exist.*
> *The next best is a leader who is loved and praised.*
> *Next comes the one who is feared.*
> *The worst one is the leader that is despised . . .*
> *The best leaders value their words, and use them sparingly.*
> *When they have accomplished their task,*
> *the people say, 'Amazing!*
> *We did it, all by ourselves!'*[3]

This emphasis on natural harmony can also be found in an early reference to market activity written in the commentaries to the *Tao Te Ching*. It states:

> When the sun stood at midday, the Divine Husbandman held
> a market. He caused the people of the world to come together

and assembled the riches of all under heaven. These they exchanged with one another and then returned home, each having found its appropriate place.[4]

The line above, 'each having found its appropriate place', implies that when things follow their natural course, everything ends up as it should be. The idea that there is a natural harmony in markets has some similarity with Adam Smith's idea of an 'invisible hand' guiding markets. Adam Smith was the father of economics in Europe, and he argued against government intervention. He believed that if market forces were left to run their own course, the result would be a more efficient and equitable use of resources. Taoists did not write on the economy in such detail but both they and Smith favoured a laissez-faire approach whereby the government refrains from action and allows natural forces to determine outcomes.

The second Chinese school of thought, Legalism, had the opposite view to leading and managing people. The Legalist view of human nature was not positive. It saw people as greedy and selfish. If they were given freedom and left to their own devices, as the Taoists suggested, there would be chaos, hence strong laws were needed to stop people from undermining social order. However, the harshness of their proposed laws and punishments have earned Legalists substantial criticism.

Legalism was the favoured philosophy of the first Chinese emperor Qin Shi Huang. The emperor had conquered a number of disparate warlords and was tasked with unifying the nation. Legalism, which offered common laws in the creation of social order, was ideal for the job. To administer the laws, the emperor created an administrative structure in which able government officials, or mandarins, would govern the country. No longer would feudal lords impose their arbitrary whims on the populace. People would be governed by consistent laws that applied to everyone.

The most influential Legalist text is the *Han Feizi*, written around 240 BC. Although the text focuses on managing a government bureaucracy, the principles can relate to any organisation which governs human activity, including business. To do this, the text provided three guiding principles: '*Fa*' (law), '*Shi*' (authority or power) and '*Shu*' (statecraft)[5].

These principles reflect a concern for the effective use of power and leadership; issues of importance to today's managers. For example, the principle '*Fa*' was based on the idea that common standards should exist and no one was above the law. This principle argued that the state should be governed by laws and standards that apply to everyone. The consequence of such a system is that everybody had a chance to succeed and those with the most talent could rise, even if they were commoners. It was a meritocracy.

The second principle, '*Shi*', focuses on authority and its locus. In particular, authority is not seated in any one individual, but the position he holds. A leader does not have personal authority, but gains it from his position. Consistent with this principle is the need for a ruler to respect the advice of his ministers and to take criticism. Leadership will be more effective when the technical expertise of ministers and advisors is acknowledged. The final principle, '*Shu*', focuses on the techniques and tactics of statecraft, and how to handle men and affairs in the political arena.

The first Chinese empire was a time when businessmen could gain significant status in Chinese society[6]. This could be seen in the career of Lü Buwei (291–235 BC), a merchant who rose to the position of chancellor to the State of Qin. During the Warring States period, Lü Buwei built up significant wealth as a travelling merchant. On one trading journey, he had the good fortune to meet Yiren, a grandson to the King of Qin state. Yiren had many brothers and was not likely to inherit the throne. Nevertheless, Lü Buwei said to himself, 'This is a rare piece of merchandise that should be saved for later.'[7]

On returning home, he said to his father, 'What is the profit on investment that one can expect from plowing fields?'

'Ten times the investment,' replied his father.

'And the return on investment in pearls and jades is how much?'

'A hundredfold.'

'And the return on investment from establishing a ruler and securing the state would be how much?'

'It would be incalculable.'

'Now if I devoted my energies to labouring in the fields, I would hardly get enough to clothe and feed myself; yet if I secure a state and establish its lord, the benefits can be passed on to future generations. I propose to go serve Prince Yiren of Qin ...'[8]

Lü Buwei then used his wealth to bribe and manipulate Yiren into a position where he became the heir apparent. When Yiren became king, Buwei was rewarded by being appointed chancellor (or prime minister). He served in this role for twelve years, after which he became implicated in a scandal and was exiled to a remote location where he committed suicide. His scheming and use of his merchant wealth did not help the image of merchants, and scholars in the subsequent Han dynasty condemned him.

When the Qin dynasty fell, Legalism fell out of favour, but the bureaucratic structure of government officials remained. However, the bureaucrats would not be trained in Legalism. They would be educated with Confucianism which, for the subsequent two thousand years, would remain the state philosophy. Not only would it shape the nature of management in government, but also the environment in which businesses operated and the strategies chosen by individual merchants. However, the influence of Confucianism on business was not always good and, at times, could be very harmful.

Confucian philosophers produced a number of texts, but the most important is the *Analects* which records the sayings of the sage Confucius (551–479 BC). In contrast to Sun Tzu who focused on war, the focus of Confucius was social harmony. Governments played an important role in this pursuit of harmony. Leaders must rule by strong moral example and cultivate the values of humaneness (*ren*), the ability to see right from wrong (*zhi*), the upholding of righteousness (*yi*), and trust (*xin*).

Most of all, governments must cultivate the value of *li*. It is difficult to translate the word *li* as it has different meanings depending on the context. It can be interpreted as 'an ideal social order with everything in its place' or 'the rites and rules of proper conduct' that contribute to that order. Confucius believed this ideal state is achieved when everyone knows their place in the natural order. If everyone lived consistent with the natural order, there would be no need for laws. A Confucian society was characterised by rituals and formal procedures in which everyone knew their place and acted appropriately. In that way, harmony was maintained.

Superiors and inferiors each knew their place and acted accordingly, but the cornerstone of society was the family. Each family member had their own role. At the head of the family was the father who bore responsibility for his family. Children, by contrast, were obligated to show respect to their parents and ancestors. This 'filial piety' was an underlying dimension of both families and business, as businesses at the time were primarily family firms.

Not everyone agreed with this approach. The Taoists thought such rituals were futile and unnatural. The Confucian world of well-defined social structures was a long way from the simple, free-flowing world espoused by the Taoists. Legalists also criticised the Confucian way. They argued that there was no moral order underlying the universe, and laws were needed to keep people in place.

The Confucians' desire for social harmony and structure came with a mindset that limited the possibilities of business. The words of Confucius are recorded in the *Analects* and his sayings constantly speak against the unbridled pursuit of wealth. The following quotations from the *Analects* show that business and the pursuit of profit had their place, but they were secondary to other values. For example, the following saying states that it is better to be poor and live properly, than to gain wealth through inappropriate means. He refers to the Tao: 'the path' and proper way to go in life.

> The Master said, 'Wealth and honor are what people want, but if they are the consequence of deviating from the way (*tao*), I would have no part of them. Poverty and disgrace are what people deplore, but if they are the consequence of staying on the way, I would not avoid them. Wherein do the exemplary persons (*junzi*) who would abandon their authoritative conduct (*ren*) warrant that name? Exemplary persons do not take leave of their authoritative conduct even for the space of a meal. When they are troubled, they certainly turn to it, as they do in facing difficulties.'

Confucius constantly stresses the importance of acting appropriately, with propriety and fairness. These qualities are much better than wealth, and indicate the hallmark of a superior person for example:

> The Master said, '. . . Exemplary persons cherish fairness; petty persons cherish the thought of gain.'
> The Master said, 'Exemplary persons (*junzi*) make their plans around the way (*tao*) and not around their sustenance . . .'

However, the following saying suggests there are appropriate ways of making money if one acts consistently with the Tao:

The Master said, [. . .] 'It is a disgrace to remain poor and without rank when the way prevails in the state; it is a disgrace to
be wealthy and of noble rank when it does not.'[9]

These statements seem relatively moderate but others are more
damming. Mencius, the greatest of Confucian scholars, viewed
merchants as 'unscrupulous men' who 'competed for profits with
the people'[10]. Such comments reflect the traditional Chinese view
that business was a low-status profession. The traditional Chinese
class structure gave status to professions depending on their
perceived value to society. At the top were the scholar-officials (or
mandarins) who were held in high esteem. Next came agricultural
peasants, in recognition of agriculture's importance as the backbone
of the economy and society. Lower in status came artisans, while
merchants were placed on the lowest rung and were often perceived
as parasites on society.

When the Han dynasty replaced the Qin dynasty in 206 BC, it
signalled a significant shift on the business environment.
Confucianism replaced Legalism and merchants experienced a
significant decline in status and freedom. When the new emperor
institutionalised his preference for agriculture and the denigration
of commerce[11], the downgrade was complete.

The government realised that some commercial activities were
needed, in particular the distribution of some vital goods to different
parts of the empire, but for this function the state chose to implement tight controls. Certain goods such as salt and tea were declared
a state monopoly. Private enterprise might participate in their distribution but only under control or licence of the government.

Markets still existed but only with consent of the government. We
can read about this early control of markets in the *Rites of Zhou*.
Written in the second century BC, this book describes how in cities
the state restricted trade to officially sanctioned marketplaces. The

government also dictated the location and functioning of markets along the main transportation routes. This high level of intervention represented a particular aspect of Chinese business that would shape business strategy. In particular, it required a businessman to cultivate relationships with government officials.

These changes inaugurated in the Han dynasty established a pattern of strong government influence in commerce that would exist for the following two thousand years. The extent of that control could vary over time. Some emperors increased control while others preferred a softer hand but, at all times, Chinese merchants knew that relationships with the government were a key determinant of their commercial strategy.

Confucian scholars did not all hold the same attitude to business. The extent to which one perceived Confucianism as being against wealth and business is very much one of individual interpretation. We can see parallels with interpretations of the Bible in which a scholar may place the emphasis on different quotations to prove their point. In general, if merchants simply circulated surplus products to areas where they were scarce, they were seen as performing a valuable role. In so doing, they filled the natural gaps between abundance and shortfall[12]. However, if merchants attempted to manipulate the market or defraud producers and consumers, as many assumed they did, they justified their social status at the lowest echelons of Chinese society.

This was a dynamic environment. The status and success of Chinese businessmen varied over time and the Confucian-trained government officials held great diversity in their views on business – this could have a huge impact on the practise of commerce. As this book progresses we will learn how businessmen could thrive in such an environment.

What is the Art of Business?

The titles of this book, *The Art of Business*, and *The Art of War* raise an important question; that is, can we define war and business as art? There are two elements that we normally relate to art. First, art normally has an aesthetic quality and there is little beauty in war. The same might be said of business. Some products and production technologies have aesthetic qualities but not all. The second definition of art is that it involves the application of a high level of skill, and by this definition both war and business can be defined as an art.

We could define business as the art of value provision. Businesses strive for profit, but they do it by creating and distributing goods and services that people value. Herein lies one of the problems with the traditional Chinese approach to business. Artisans and merchants were considered to be of the lowest social status, yet artisans created the products that people value, and merchants were the ones who distributed them. Any restrictions placed on their activities reduced the opportunity to give people more value, and enhance their quality of life.

The Chinese long suffered for this view. The focus was on social harmony, which is a good thing, but the restrictions that accompanied it limited the ability of the Chinese to achieve their potential. It would be a thousand years after the Han dynasty (206 BC) came to power before the economy began to show its potential and business people had the opportunity truly to practise their art.

This book begins in the Tang dynasty (AD 618–907); a time when these restrictions began to be lifted and businesses could provide new values to Chinese people. This book then follows Chinese business through time, examining how they made money in different periods and different environments. In so doing, we examine the techniques of those who succeeded and failed in the art of Chinese business.

CHAPTER 2

The Tang and Song Commercial Revolution

....

Off to match wits for a few hours at the Market
Numerous as clouds are the lodges and the stores
They bring hemp cloth and paper – mulberry paper
Or drive before them chickens and suckling pigs
This way and that lie piles of brooms and dustpans
So many domestic trifles they cannot all be listed.[1]

The extract above was written by the monk Tao Ch'ien in his poem 'on the way to the Kuei-tsung Monastery'. The poem captures the growing excitement of markets that he personally observed during his lifetime. Peasant farmers were becoming petty entrepreneurs, each one expanding the range of goods available to consumers. This was the time when an economic structure evolved providing wealth greater than any other region in the world, and the average Chinese enjoyed a level of prosperity that other people could only dream of.

During the Tang (AD 618–907) and Song (AD 960–1279) dynasties, China underwent a commercial revolution. An environment was created that made it possible for people to become entrepreneurs and improve their livelihood. Several developments contributed to this, but perhaps the most important was the development of internal transportation systems that enabled merchants to trade goods across the country, in particular the Grand Canal. The initial construction of the canal dates to the Warring States period (475–221 BC), but it was not until AD 735 that improvements in the canal enabled the large-scale movement of grain from the south to the north of the country. The Grand Canal was not one continuous waterway but a series of short canals that linked together existing waterways[2]. By linking these waterways, the government was able to transport taxes, officials, troops, documents and supplies to the north.

Although completed for use by the government, private enterprise soon recognised the canal's potential as a trade connection. Goods produced in the south, such as rice, tea, silk and textiles, could be shipped in large quantities to the markets in the north, and vice versa. Large cities grew on the banks of the canal, each one acting as a transfer port for the north–south trade. The importance of the canal to the economy can be gauged by the tax records from the Song dynasty. These records show that China's key commercial centres were based on the canal[3].

As important as the Grand Canal was, it was not the only waterway used by traders, and a number of other routes co-existed and fed the canal. Many of these minor waterways connected to the Grand Canal acting as feeders from other regions. These transport links reflected an economy mobilising its natural resources to build a prosperous society. As a Tang dynasty commentator noted:

> There is no commandery or county in the southeast in which communications by water are lacking. Therefore most of the Empire's profits from trade depend on the use of boats[4].

Water transport made it easier to sell goods, and a local producer could obtain higher prices if they sold in a distant market. This could be seen from the price of grain that varied depending on the access to water transport. At inland regions which had no access, 100 shi of grain (approximately 7,000kg) could sell for fourteen strings of cash, but sellers in regions with water connections would sell at twenty[5].

As water transport became more common, innovations were introduced that further reduced the cost of transport. These innovations included engineering techniques for the construction of locks and canals and the dredging of rivers. Specialised ships were built that could overcome problems in regional waters, while management techniques also became more efficient. The consequence of these innovations was an ever-improving transportation system, and an increasingly efficient market. A writer from the Song dynasty noted:

> The rivers and lakes are linked together, so that one can go everywhere by means of them. But when a boat leaves its home port there are no obstacles to its planning a journey of 10,000 li (approximately 3,100 miles). Every year the common people use all the grain that is surplus to their requirements for seeds and food for trading. Large merchants gather what the lesser households have. Little boats engage in joint operations with the greater vessels as the latter's dependents, going back and forth selling grain in order to clear a solid profit.[6]

As the cost of transportation fell, it made it possible for more suppliers to enter the market, while those already in the market benefitted from reduced costs. Water transportation costs in the eleventh century were one fifth what they had been in the eighth century. A study by William Liu at the Hong Kong University of Science and Technology revealed the extent of this decline. He found that if a Tang dynasty merchant wanted to transport 100 jin of goods (approximately 65 kilograms) along 45 kilometres of water, he would have paid an average rate of 150 wen if he was moving upstream and 50 wen in the opposite direction. By AD 1202, the rates had declined to 30 wen for an upstream journey and 10 for a downstream journey of the same length[7].

This expansion of commercial activity ran contrary to an outlook that had dominated China since the Han dynasty. For centuries, commerce had been seen as something 'fundamentally undesirable'[8]. However, in the Tang dynasty, the government realised that commerce couldn't be supressed, and if kept under control could contribute substantially to state revenues. The more commercial activity occurred, the more tax they would earn, so the government acquired a new attitude to commerce and encouraged productivity.

Other policy changes by the government contributed to this economic boom. Prior to this time, taxation was collected via a poll tax, hence the state needed to know where all taxpayers were and forbid migration. This included merchants, as a travelling merchant lacked a fixed residence, which meant that they were not taxed. This dramatically reduced business activity. If a merchant could not freely move, it would prove a significant handicap to the distribution of goods.

These restrictions ended in 755, with the replacement of the poll tax. Officials decided to raise revenue from other sources, in particular taxing commerce (and state monopolies on salt and alcohol). A network of internal custom stations was set up around the country to tax merchants transporting goods, while a number of superintendencies were created to tax foreign trade[9]. This represented a significant change in government outlook from restricting trade to encouraging it, and a more positive environment for business.

Another change in policy came when the government undertook to increase the money supply. Prior to this time, trade was done on the basis of barter, as there was a limited amount of money available. This changed when the government injected greater volumes of money into the economy, which made it easier for people to trade. The Song government minted the largest number of bronze coins in Chinese history: a total of 193.4 million strings of them[10].

A money economy has huge advantages over one based on barter. For barter to occur, it requires a person to have what someone else wants, and they in turn must have what the other desires. Only then can an equal exchange occur. In a money economy, sellers and buyers have more options. With money, goods can be sold to one person, and the money earned can be used to buy from someone else. This dramatically increased the trading options. Money had the added advantage that it could be stored, which increased the times when business could occur. People could sell their goods and hold on to the money until they were ready to use it. When everyone recognises the value of money, a sale could occur at any time.

Before the Tang dynasty, a farmer's production was based on self-sufficiency, whereby they grew the goods they needed for themselves. This clearly limited what products they had access to. With the development of water transportation, it was possible for farmers to sell any surplus stock they produced to distant markets. The farmers soon discovered what products provided the best returns, and with the money they earned, they could buy the goods that they had trouble producing themselves. They began to specialise in a small number of crops that they produced best. With everyone focusing on what they did best, the nation experienced a leap in agricultural production and economic growth.

Different types of markets appeared around the empire. Rural markets were held in small villages. These markets were not permanent, but occasional events that occurred on a regular basis. Peasant farmers would come to the market and exchange their surplus output with other peasants. Consequently, the goods traded at these markets were those produced in the local area. This might include grain, rice, poultry or tea. A verse from a poem that circulated in the Song and Yuan dynasties celebrates this localised enterprise:

This small market –
People within bundles of tea or salt
Chickens cackling, dogs barking
Firewood being exchanged for rice
And fishes bartered for wine[11].

By the eleventh century, 20,606 rural markets were in existence[12]. Some of these markets grew into centres of inter-regional trade, particularly if they were on a major transportation route. At the larger markets, commerce became more firmly established with permanent shops for grain, wine and other commodities, while inns catered for merchants who came from other regions to buy and sell[13].

Of course, disputes occurred, particularly if someone felt short-changed, and it became necessary for some level of supervision. The largest markets had a large organisation of officials supervising them. For example, at Ch'ang-an, supervision consisted of a market director and two assistants who were all ranked officials. To assist them, their staff included a managing clerk, three store-keepers, seven scribes, two intendents and one bookkeeper[14]. They administered strict laws on market operations. The extent and sophistication of these commercial laws is remarkable when one considers that, at the same time, Europe was living in the Dark Ages. For example, Tang Code 26, article 32 was written to ensure that traders do not use false weights and measures to cheat clients. It states:

In all cases where private persons have themselves made measures of capacity, steelyards and measures of length which are inaccurate, and have used them in the market, the punishment shall be a beating of fifty strokes[15].

Another law, Code 26, article 30 was written to ensure that the products sold were not faulty or of poor quality. It states:

Any person who manufactures utensils and such things as hempen or silk cloth which are fragile, not made of the appropriate materials, are short length or narrow in width, and sells them, shall be liable to a flogging of sixty strokes[16].

A common strategy used by merchants to increase income was to acquire market power which enabled them to manipulate market prices. Once again, a law existed to cover this. Entitled 'prevention of unfair trading practices', Code 26, article 33 states:

In all cases where the buyers and sellers cannot reach a settlement, and an attempt is made to monopolise the market and prevent outsiders from buying, or to attempt to fix prices unfairly, making cheap goods dear when selling, and expensive goods cheap when buying, in the hope of deceiving the customers, or if any attempt is made to confuse the market with an eye to the merchants' reaping the profit for themselves, they shall be liable to a flogging of eighty blows[17].

There is no doubt that there were holes in the implementation of these laws, but the sophistication of the commercial–legal environment is striking, particularly when one compares it to Europe and other parts of the world at the same time. Such laws sought to reduce exploitation, but one positive effect was to increase confidence in the use of the market, so that people could buy and sell in confidence.

So advanced were the Chinese that they also established laws to control the governing officials. For example, at times officials were required to fix prices to reduce the chance of profiteering. However, Code 26, article 31 was written to ensure that the officials did not exploit this process. It states:

If the market officials are unjust in fixing the prices of commodities, they shall be liable to punishment as for pecuniary malfeasance to the extent to which they have raised or lowered prices. If as a result they themselves have profited thereby, they shall be liable to a punishment under the provisions on robbery to the same amount[18].

By today's standards, some of the regulations might seem excessive. For example, to help control the market, traders in similar commodities were grouped together in a row. Not only did these rows designate the location of products, but their common location facilitated organisation for people from the same industry. They were a prototype guild for those trades, and the Chinese word for row, *hang*, became the Chinese word for 'guild'. However, at this time, they lacked the complexity and functions of the guilds that would appear later in the Ming dynasty.

Smaller markets would not have a large official organisation to oversee them. They would instead have a market director whose job was to perform the same functions. These included the registration of all shops, inspection of weights and measures, ensuring product quality, preventing unfair price fixing and registering certain types of goods such as livestock and slaves. It was important to verify that no free person was being sold as a slave[19].

A description of a smaller market operating in the Tang dynasty has been preserved and provides a vivid eyewitness account of its operation and the attitude of those involved. The description was written by Liu Yu-hsi, a Confucian-trained writer and official. It may have an anti-business bias, but nevertheless is of great interest to the business historian. The description[20] repeated below was written in the year 808. Officials were not allowed to enter markets, so Liu watched down on the market from the town gate towers.

The first section notes that the need to organise different trades into rows also existed in the smaller towns. It then describes the wide range of goods available including slaves, cloth, furniture, and goods that came from foreigners (outer barbarians) to the market:

Notices proclaimed the names of the various rows and sections, and made known the prices and named the commodities on sale. Mingled among them were commodities produced among the outer barbarians. There were tethering places for horse and cattle. There were pens for slaves. The cloth covered boxes for silks contained both patterned and plain woven materials. Among the tables and sets of shelves there were both carved and lacquered ones, and others were unadorned and substantial. Among the round and square basketware there were both black and white, both delicate and sturdy pieces.

Those whose profession was providing food set out their hot dishes and laid out cakes and dumplings surrounded by fragrant smells. The wine-sellers set up their banners advertising their wines, and washed up their wine cups and bowls with shining faces. The butchers set up their platters for fat, and carved up the carcases of pigs and sheep in a thick red atmosphere of blood. The product of flower and fruit, game taken in the hunt, birds and beasts were mixed together, the products of land and water were intermingled.

The next paragraph describes the people who came to the market and the strategies used; strategies we will expand on in the next chapter:

Every sort of person came in their flocks, innumerable people enter the narrow alleyways between the stalls and then split up again. There were some who hoarded up goods, waiting to get the right price. Others carried the deeds for sale for goods and sought to sell them. Some were out to take any chance to make a gain, some had made their profit and were out to enjoy themselves. There were seated hawkers sitting humbly and respectfully, walking peddlers hastening along.

In the next paragraph, we see the importance of the laws promoting fair trade and the need for enforcement. The references to defamation and swindling are reminiscent of Sun Tzu's *The Art of War* and its emphasis on deception. However, some of the observations seem to go beyond what Liu might see and hear from his tower. If the merchants were engaging in these behaviours, we might expect their conversations to be at a level that clients would not be able to hear them. Given that the market was full of 'flocks' of people, it is somewhat surprising that he heard these conversations from his position at the market gate:

Hearts intent on price are excited. Covetous eyes do not shut for an instant. Fellow merchants in charge of contracts, groups devoted to restricting trade within their own circle, conclude agreements between this one and that, and push the prices up. Feigning to do good, they cause trouble by their crafty words. Fair weight is ruined by their crafty hands. They trade on the difference of the minutest amounts in weight. Evil gossip grates on the ear. Defamation and swindling thrive. Treacherous behaviour is everywhere to be seen. They raise a frightful hubbub, stir up the dust and dirt, emanate a rank stink like goats, pile together head-cloths and sandals. Snapping and gnawing at one another they congregate . . . By the time their business is finished and they return home, the suns glow has reached the West . . . On this day, leaning on the parapet, I watched them carefully, pondering how their profit and loss were so intimately interdependent, and speedily set it all down in this essay.

There may be another explanation for this description in that the author was simply presenting a conventional Confucian stereotype of traders. Nevertheless, the fair trading laws were introduced for a reason, and there is no doubt that each transaction would be meticulously wrangled to maximise income.

THE ART OF SONG COMMERCE

The water transport routes tied the different regions of China into a national market of diverse climates and growing conditions. Farmers learned that the market would reward them if they worked hard, so increased their output and welcomed innovations that appeared over this period. This included the increased use of fertilizer, oxen plough and other farm implements[21]. Some farms practised double cropping, wheat together with rice, while significant attention was given to irrigation and water control. A particularly important change was the introduction of drought resistant Champa rice from Vietnam, which had the benefit of providing more than one crop a year. In a thirteenth century proclamation to encourage agriculture, it was stated:

In Wu, the people open up the waste lands and swampy depressions for the cultivation of rice of moderate gluten content and they also plant vegetables, wheat, hemp and beans. When they cultivate they do not neglect their dykes; When they reap, they do not overlook the boundaries between the fields. But in Yu-chang they grow mostly Champa rice of low gluten content, either the 80-day, the 100-day or the

120-day variety, from any of which a harvest may be had in a few months . . . Thus, the farmers of Wu are distinguished for their application[22].

The region to undergo the most dramatic agricultural transformation during this time was the lower Yangtze. Prior to AD 750, the region was sparsely populated. The lower delta region was prone to flooding and required significant investment in water control to turn these swamps into productive farmland. In the Tang and Song dynasties, this occurred with substantial investment in land conversion. Government records show that between 1070 and 1076 alone, 8,686 irrigation projects were completed. The mid and lower Yangtze received the majority of these (5,193 projects). Most of these projects were either partially funded by the government or sponsored by wealthy landlords who had an interest in increased output[23].

The Song government saw the benefits of this transformation and took an active role in improving productivity. For example, in 1020 the emperor Zhenzong ordered the imperial library to print a classical text on agriculture, *Qimin yaoshu* by Jia Sixie, for distribution around the country. Such intervention helped expand productivity across China.

By the time of the Song dynasty, the swampy lowlands had been transformed so dramatically that they were now the grain basket for the country[24]. From that point on the area known as Jiangnan (south of the Yangtze) was a principal engine driving the Chinese economy. The importance of this region and the process of transformation is captured in a document written in the Southern Song period. The author states that, if the principal cities of this area:

. . . have a good harvest then the whole empire has a sufficiency, but it is also true that, because of the multiplying population, then new lands being brought under cultivation, reed-swamps and thickets being opened up each year and the dyked fields spreading ever wider, even if they do not enjoy a good harvest they still obtain enough to sustain them for several years[25].

The economic growth in the lower Yangtze was impressive and would have inspired envy in any other nation in the world. However, it was not the star in the Chinese crown. That position belonged to the capital city, Kaifeng, whose position at the end of the Grand Canal made it the hub on which the Chinese wheel turned.

KAIFENG: THE HUB ON WHICH THE ECONOMY TURNED

At the beginning of the tenth century, a decision was made to locate the capital at Kaifeng. The new location was based on the confluence of four major waterways, the most important of which was the Grand Canal. Through these waterways, Kaifeng sucked in resources from around the empire to support the city's massive population. By 1078, the city's population was estimated to be somewhere between 750,000 and one million. It had grown fifteen-fold from its pre-capital days in AD 742. A population of this size needs substantial food imports to sustain it, and it has been suggested that 80 per cent of its food requirements were met from produce arriving through the Grand Canal, with other supplies arriving on the other waterways linked to the city[26].

The capital was home to the emperor, with his retinue of concubines, eunuchs and servants. It was also home to the country's bureaucracy. The regular officials and subordinate clerical workers probably constituted the largest professional group in the city[27]. The next sizeable group was the military. In 1078, there were at least 150,000 troops stationed in the city, and at times the figure might be twice that. When the logistics personnel were added, it has been estimated that half a million people living in the capital were directly dependent on the state for their living.

To feed this population, a substantial volume of food needed to be transported to the city. However, the requirements of the population were not restricted to basic foodstuffs. They also required clothing, housing, drink, and fuel for cooking and heating. Each of these consumer demands provided an opportunity for an entrepreneur to establish a successful business. For example, the locals needed entertainment, so the eleventh century saw the establishment of theatres and taverns within the city – eight amusement centres were created which could accommodate several thousand customers at a time[28].

There are few artworks that capture business and economic activity from the past, but a Song dynasty artist by the name of Zhang Zeduan (1085–1145) painted a scroll that captured the various forms of business that existed in the capital at the time. The scroll is considered China's most important painting and is often referred to as 'China's *Mona Lisa*'. It is sometimes called the *Qingming Scroll*, but its full name is *Along the River During the Qingming Festival*. The Qingming festival is a time when the Chinese honour their ancestors and visit their graves.

The section above shows camels carrying a cargo through the city gates. Taverns and shops have their doors open to entice customers inside.

The Qingming scroll illustrates a range of commercial activities and the importance of water transportation. In this section, cargo ships line the waterway. In the bottom right corner, a woman and child engage with a peddler selling banners. In the middle of the picture is a wine shop, and on the left is a restaurant.

The scroll is 5.25 metres (5.74 yards) long and scans activity from the borders of the city to the inner city. The importance of transportation can be seen with twenty-eight boats pictured on the canal, sixty draft animals, twenty vehicles and nine sedan chairs featured on the full scroll. Donkeys and mules carry coal through the streets which also abound with entertainers. A number of trades are represented including bookkeepers, pawnbrokers, metalworkers, carpenters and doctors.

The entertainment industry is represented by jugglers, actors, fortune-tellers, waiters and innkeepers. Such businesses provided food, alcohol and courtesans. To supply the taverns, entrepreneurs established breweries. Such was the demand for beer that, in 1077, more than 566,000 bushels of rice were used in its production. This quantity could be achieved because of the efficiency of the nation's water transportation bringing rice to the city. In this way, demand in the capital created a supply chain comprised of entrepreneurs adding value at each link of the chain.

Breweries were just one of many industries stimulated by demand in the capital. Paper making, printing, alum making, shipbuilding, salt processing, quicksilver and cinnabar production flourished in this market and reached a scale of output not seen in any other country until the eighteenth century[29].

The extent to which Kaifeng dominated the economy can be seen from the government's taxation records. In 1077, Kaifeng produced 402,379 strings of commercial tax revenue, substantially more than any other city[30]. The next best city was Hangzhou, the commercial giant in the bustling lower Yangtze. However, it only generated 82,173 strings, one fifth that of Kaifeng. The capital city was the hub on which the Chinese economy turned, as this description from 1137 shows:

> There are numerous commercial transactions at the capital conducted by merchants from every part of the country, and the city is therefore reputed for its wealth and population. Most of those who possess capital engage in stockpiling and storage, pawn-broking or trading in ships. How could they permit their accumulated wealth to lie idle, or buy gold for hoarding at home?[31]

THE COAL AND IRON INDUSTRIES

The most dynamic industrial advance during this time occurred in the extraction and refining of metallic ores. The Chinese metallurgy industries produced output at a level that Europeans wouldn't see for another seven hundred years (in the Industrial Revolution). For example, in 1067, the Chinese industry produced 331,500 tons of iron, copper lead and tin for construction, production and military uses[32].

Once again, it was the capital city that determined the industry's growth. The region around Kaifeng was blessed with fuel and ore deposits, but it was not the only one with such resources. Many regions in China had the same endowment of coal and iron ore, but they did not experience the industrial growth of those close to Kaifeng. It was the growing demand for ferrous metal products in the capital that drove the industry and provided the impetus for entrepreneurs to invest in capital and new technologies.

Until this time, iron mining and smelting was not highly organised, principally because the market was too limited to facilitate a higher level of organisation. There were few full-time employees in the industry. Mines and foundries were operated by groups of peasants whose normal job was farming. They would only work in the mines and foundries in the idle season between the autumn harvest and spring ploughing when there was little to do on the farm. This meant that, at most, fifty-seven days of the year from December to January were spent split between mining and smelting. It was small-scale production using a small blast furnace capable of producing no more than half a ton of iron per day.

These peasant groups provided the iron for village blacksmiths who made the utensils, ploughshares, shovels and other tools for farmers. An official investigation recorded this form of production during the Southern Song (1127–1279):

> most of the [mine-]worker households of the various villages consider plowing and sowing to be [their] occupation. Intermittently, when there is leisure from agriculture, ten or twenty households band together and enter a pit. Sometimes there is a surplus, and sometimes [their efforts] result in failure[33].

At the time this was written, the industry around Kaifeng had already undergone a transformation. The reason for this transformation was the huge demand for iron that existed in the capital. A casual labour force with low-capacity furnaces simply could not produce the quantity or quality of iron needed in this market. To meet this demand, iron needed to be mined all year round. Similarly, foundries needed to operate continuously with a full-time, not casual, workforce. This created opportunities for entrepreneurs to establish profitable businesses. In the process, they became very wealthy.

To commence a business like this requires significant capital. At the mines, substantial investment was needed to fund drainage equipment, explosives, and ballista-like devices that raised the fragmented rock to the surface. Funding was also required to purchase the sledgehammers, chisels, picks, shovels and wheelbarrows used by the labourers who worked the diggings.

We do not know the background of the entrepreneurs who made these investments, but Robert Hartwell, who studied the industry of this time, suggests that the investment was probably undertaken by the owners of the land on which the ore lay. They became ironmasters and employed the workers, thereby changing the industry from a casual activity into something resembling a modern industry.

Hartwell also suggested another way that investors may have ended up owning these plants. He puts it that the peasant groups may have continued to operate their local mines and foundries but came in debt to creditors who made them advances. It is possible the peasant miners needed funds to buy new tools to help increase output. However, if they could not meet their repayments, the creditors were in a position to take ownership of the enterprise, and the peasants, who once owned the facility, now became paid employees.

Demand from the Kaifeng market enabled entrepreneurs to invest in larger plants which could be operated continuously. In so doing, businesses benefitted from economies of scale. When combined with technological innovations, this facilitated a substantial decrease in costs. Robert Hartwell compared the price of iron to that of staple grain (rice) in Szechwan province in the years 997 and 1080. He found that in 997 the price ratio was 632 for iron compared to 100 for grain, but by 1080 the ratio was 177 to 100. Effectively, iron had become three and a half times cheaper.

Compared to a peasant-run foundry which produced less than twenty tons of iron a year, the new enterprises were giants, averaging 1,287 tons each year in the 1070s[34]. As a consequence national output soared 285 per cent between 998 and 1078. Surprisingly, there was actually a decline in the number of production centres. However, what happened a thousand years ago is consistent with studies of modern business. Recent studies of American industries reveal that when an industry grows, smaller businesses that cannot match the economies of scale of larger businesses cease operations, and the industry becomes concentrated among a smaller number of giant companies. This is exactly what happened in the Song dynasty iron industry.

The iron ore produced was taken to the capital where metalworking plants transformed it into products that would be consumed locally or exported to other parts of China. A large part of that demand came from the military and its need for armaments. Weapon making was conducted by official arsenals which consumed a significant amount of the locally produced iron. At the end of the tenth century, the two major armament works employed a staff of almost 8,000 to produce an annual output of 32,000 swords, suits of armour, lances and other weapons[35]. There was also a bow-and-arrow works which produced over 16,500,000 bows, arrows and arrowheads each year. Orders of this size were for regular years. If the military needed to undertake a specific campaign, special orders would be added to these quotas.

The government also used iron to fabricate non-military items. Five thousand men were employed in state workshops that produced items as diverse as lamps, hammers, bells, cymbals, hinges, saws, drum fittings, lamps, locks, boilers, pins, nails and needles. The government also needed to produce coins to maintain the money supply and by 1078, the iron coin mints were producing 150,000 strings of two cash coins each year, cast from 1,350 tons of iron. However, the government did not have a monopoly on the manufacture of iron products. At least three privately owned businesses have been identified that specialised in the manufacture of iron products, and there were probably many more.

Much of the output was exported to other parts of China. The products were taken to distant regions on the same waterways that brought grain, clothing and other materials to the city. Through this process, the northern industrial enterprises buttressed Kaifeng's role as the centre of a national market system with webs spread out in all directions.

This growth had some negative consequences. In particular, the demand for timber to create charcoal resulted in massive deforestation. Not only was this harmful for the environment, but the industry was losing a vital fuel supply. The industry responded to this by changing fuel sources from charcoal to coke made from nearby coal deposits.

A Song Dynasty Entrepreneur

For business people, the environment in Song China was highly favourable to investment and starting a business. The state provided a stable money supply, efficient transportation networks, and a large army insured domestic peace and external security. Under such conditions, entrepreneurs had confidence to invest large sums of money and create the enterprises that made China the strongest economy in the world.

We have record of one industrialist from this period, although he operated further south[36]. His name was Wang Ko. The report says that he came from a well-to-do family for he received a Confucian education and passed his examinations. His biography states that after an argument with his brother, he 'left home with nothing but an umbrella'. However, he somehow had the resources to buy a mountain covered with timber. He used the timber to produce charcoal and also began to produce iron with ore which presumably lay on his property. The region had long been known to possess iron ore.

He initially employed local farmers which suggests he was operating under the old industry structure in which farmers would make charcoal in their off-season to gain extra income. However, Wang Ko soon created more modern enterprises. He set up two foundries which together employed around five hundred workers. The workers were defined as vagabonds who would have welcomed the employment that Wang Ko provided.

While Wang Ko personally managed one foundry, he appointed a manager to oversee the second one. His choice for the position was Ch'ien Ping-te, who came from an old gentry family that had fallen on hard times and needed the employment. The use of local gentry would have given his business the added advantages of status and connections.

Wang Ko appears to be an enterprising industrialist, establishing a secure supply of raw materials, charcoal and ore, before establishing two foundries. He invested in management and established a full-time labour force of more than five hundred workers as well as a number of part-timers. He also invested in other enterprises, including a lake which employed 'several hundred' families to fish. It is assumed he either sold the fish or licences to fish.

He also gained ownership of a wine shop after a legal dispute with the previous owner. However, it was said that his success in this enterprise was not because of good business methods. The shop had a state monopoly licence, and it was by exploiting the power of this monopoly that the shop made a profit.

It is at this point that his money-making activities diverge from that which we normally associate with sound commercial practice. He created a private armed guard which he used to terrorise and blackmail local officials. This, together with his contacts in the gentry, may have helped buffer him from extortion by the officials. He placed importance on cultivating *guanxi* (relationships) with people he considered important, but his methods meant he was in danger of creating powerful enemies. By his subordinates, he was described as 'haughty'.

His tactics seem more akin to something that you would read in *The Art of War*, but such strategies have limited use in business, as he created enemies. In 1181, it all came crashing down. His downfall began when he entrusted two soldiers who had served in his son's private guard, to deliver a letter to a retired army officer who now ran a business. However, the soldiers held a grudge against Wang Ko and took the letter to the provincial government. The content of the letter suggested he was preparing for a rebellion.

An order was issued for Wang Ko's arrest, but local officials were scared to act. Such was his ability to intimidate that soldiers would not obey the orders they were given. Eventually, a commander was sent with ten soldiers to arrest Wang, who responded by bribing the commander. However, the exchange of bank notes was witnessed by one of the soldiers, who raised the alarm. A brawl ensued with most of the soldiers killed and the commander taken prisoner. Wang Ko then mobilised his workers for an attack on the city. He successfully entered the city, but his men rebelled against him. Wang was caught and executed.

The life of Wang Ko serves as a reminder that, to have long-term success, we should ignore the Art of War and follow the Art of Business. In the next chapter, we consider some of the strategies used by successful businessmen at this time.

CHAPTER 3

How Did Merchants Make Money? – The Time-Space Dimension

....

It is human nature for everyone to desire riches. Even peasants, artisans and merchants all scheme away at night and day in search of profit[1].

ARBITRAGE

In any business, profit is the difference between revenue and expenses. In simple terms, this means a merchant needs to sell his goods at a price higher than it cost to buy them. For a merchant in Song China, the best opportunity to do this came from buying goods in a region where they were plentiful and the price low, then transporting them to a region where the goods were scarce and the price high. This was the business model made possible by the Grand Canal and other transport innovations.

Merchants made their money from the difference in prices, less the costs of distribution[2]. It is an example of what economists call arbitrage, that is taking advantage of the price variations in different markets, but this raises the question, 'how did merchants know which markets would give the highest prices?' One writer of the time, Hung Mai, suggested they sought guidance from local deities. Speaking of a group in Jiangsi, he notes they:

... devoutly believe in the great magical powers of the Violet Lady Spirit, for she always informs them of profits to be made from forthcoming events. Sometimes she will tell them that tea will be expensive down the river, and so suitable for dealing in; or else that there will be a shortage of rice in some place or another, to which a cargo of it should be taken. They invariably do as she says and make substantial profits[3].

The merchant manuals published in the Ming and Qing dynasties are more earthbound in their advice to merchants. They stressed the importance of knowledge and experience. A merchant needed to develop capabilities that enabled them to understand markets. They did not need to know all markets, just the markets in which they dealt. And it was important that they restricted themselves to markets that they had knowledge of. For example, the Chinese merchant manual *Solutions for Merchants* states:

If you do not know it, do not buy it. Keep to your own trade. As for normal trade and familiar goods, although the profit is small, and supply of goods is irregular, you must not lightly change and abandon (your original trade). If you suddenly take up a new trade, you will not be able to completely judge the quality of the goods. The prices (too) will be difficult to determine[4].

This advice bears strong similarity to the advice that the American billionaire Warren Buffet gave in the twenty-first century. Buffet advised business people to keep to their 'circle of competence'. It didn't matter how big their circle was – what mattered was that they stay within it. When a merchant entered into unfamiliar territory, they were exposing themselves to factors of which they had little knowledge.

The importance of knowing your market can be seen in the following comment by the Ming dynasty official, Zhang Han.

He noted the ability that successful merchants had in reading and exploiting markets:

> The merchants boast that their knowledge and ability are sufficient to get them anything they want. They set their minds on monopolising the operations of change in the natural world and scheme to exploit the natural transformations of man and animal. They shift with the times; when they offer their goods for sale, they control the prices. Tallying it all up, they do not let a hundredth part slip by[5].

Merchants were well aware of the importance of commercial information. The arbitrage strategy required a knowledge of what regions produced a good and in what regions demand exceeded supply. However, they also needed an understanding of changes in the market. They needed to know what caused the price of a good to change and how long that price change would last. For example, 'did the price of a commodity go up because a large region was struck by drought, or was it just a small part of the region and more supplies would soon be available?'

If a merchant had knowledge of the factors that drove prices and supplies, they could make better decisions on how much of a product to carry and what prices would generate a profit. This was confirmed in the merchant manual *The Merchant's Guide* which noted that a merchant must learn about the 'flow of goods everywhere' so he can 'know the information and opportunities in time and know what to do and what not to do'[6].

The information on changing market conditions needed to be accurate and up to date. A business manual entitled *Essential Business*, published in the Qing dynasty, stated that a merchant needed to investigate the source of all market changes. It was important to determine that the change was real and not the result of another merchant manipulating information or disseminating false information.

Merchants developed distribution networks that were not just sources of goods and customers, but also sources of information. However, this was an age when news travelled slowly. A merchant could not telephone a colleague for the latest news. They had to take what information they could and analyse it carefully. The *Essential Business* advised shopkeepers to occasionally leave their shops and visit other tradesmen to gain up-to-date information. They then needed to determine the source of that information and how reliable it was[7].

Of course, even the wisest of merchants could be hit by circumstances beyond their control. Unexpected changes in the environment could bring either fortune or famine depending on the nature of that change and the extent to which the merchant was exposed. For example, the twelfth-century scholar Lu Tsu-ch'ien explained that:

> If there is no rain for ten days and the streams run dry and merchant's ships cannot come through, then the price of rice rises abruptly, and great and small will make a clamor, just as in a year of dearth[8].

In such situations, a merchant holding stock will benefit from the price rise. On the other hand, a merchant waiting for stock to arrive will be thrown into a panic. Seen in this light, praying to gods for assistance can be seen as a worthwhile investment. There was only so much that a merchant could control; the rest was down to fate.

Transporting goods in thirteenth-century China was full of risk, either from crime, natural impediment or changing market conditions. Unsurprisingly, the merchants looked for divine guidance before undertaking such ventures. The Venetian merchant, Marco Polo, witnessed this when he toured China. He recorded how:

> If anyone proposes to embark on some important enterprise or to travel somewhere on a trading venture or on other business, or has in mind some other project whose outcome he would like to know, he will consult the astrologers, telling them the year, month, hour and minute of his nativity . . . then the soothsayer, having ascertained under which constellation and which planet he was born, will predict in due sequence all that is to happen to him on his travels and what fortune, good or bad, will attend his undertaking[9].

If the astrologer reported back bad news, the merchant would delay his enterprise until conditions were more favourable. Other strategies available to a merchant included reducing their exposure to any one event, or diversifying their investments. While fate and luck were recognised as playing important roles in determining where a person ended up, more important was hard work. The author of *The Merchant's Guide*, Wu Zhongfu, phrased it succinctly when he said:

> Whether you become extremely wealthy depends on your fate; whether you become modestly wealthy depends on your effort[10].

If a merchant worked hard, he could become modestly wealthy and live a good life, but fate would determine how wealthy he became. However, if a merchant did not work or develop expertise, they would not enjoy the benefits of wealth, as *Solutions for Merchants* states:

Wealth comes from hard work, poverty from laziness ... Heaven confers rank according to talent. People who are capable can make a fortune for their family[11].

SPECULATION

A merchant's skills were not limited to knowing 1. What to buy, 2. How much to buy, and 3. At what price to trade. It also involved knowing when to buy and sell. There was a strong temporal element to trade. The importance of timing was emphasised in the manual *Shishang yaolan*, which stated 'do not mistake the time, when to do trade'. Given the constant flows of goods and variations in prices, the time which a merchant chooses to act could significantly affect financial outcomes. As the *Shishang leiyao* ('*Essentials for Gentry and Merchants*') states:

There is much uncertainty in business. Prices are not steady. One needs to know when to buy and sell[12].

An experienced merchant knew that trade was characterised by unexpected events. They needed to expect the unexpected. The solution was, once again, acquiring capabilities in the trade so that they could better read the market. If one acquires this knowledge and skill, one will know when to trade. This will enable you not just to survive, but to prosper in a fluctuating market.

Price variability was a common feature of the economy, and all the merchant manuals stressed that a merchant needed to deal with these fluctuations. For example, the following quotations come from three different manuals, but all recognise the role played by temporal fluctuations:

When goods become extremely expensive, then they must become inexpensive again. This is the ultimate principle[13].

. . . goods have their flourishing and waning and prices are not set. You must recognise that in a depressed market, upswings will also occur. When market prices are high, downturns are concealed. When prices begin to rise, anticipate a good time for selling[14].

No item will remain expensive for over 100 days and no item will remain cheap for 100 days . . . when things reach an extreme, they will return the other way[15].

Some merchants took advantage of the price differences that occurred over time, placing it at the core of their business strategy. For example, many merchants took advantage of the fact that agricultural products would be cheap at harvest time when they were plentiful, but became more expensive as the year progressed and stock ran out. They exploited the time differences in markets by storing product, then when the price rose, released the stock and reaped the higher profits. For this strategy to be effective, the cost of storage must be less than the expected rise in price. For example, one writer explained how on one occasion . . .

Powerful families monopsonistically purchased the entire quantity with the object of waiting until grain prices rise next year, when they will be able to make a good profit from their stocks. They did not let the poor people buy any[16].

Rich merchants could use their market power to deny the poor. It was practices such as this that attracted criticism from Confucian scholars and officials. The scholar-officials wanted to see resources shared more equitably. Those with the resources to store rice could take advantage of price fluctuations that occurred over time. It was an example of the phrase 'the rich get richer'. By contrast, peasants held no storage facilities and had to sell at harvest time when the market was flooded with the new crop, and the price was at its lowest. Furthermore, they may have pressure to sell quickly to pay taxes or repay debt. This gave the merchants who bought their stock significant market power. It also exposed them to ridicule and, for many, justified their position at the bottom of the social order.

Some merchants would exploit price fluctuations by making credit available. They would approach farmers prior to the harvest when the farmer's funds were running low. The merchants then offered to sell them goods on credit. This placed the farmers in debt to the merchants who then returned at harvest time to collect the harvest at favourable prices:

> A good harvest would enable the people to be self sufficient except for the fact that great merchants would come prior to this time with other goods for sale and then, the moment the grain came on the market, make a great profit from it[17].

> Every year rich merchants would first lend salt and tea to the people and then in the autumn they would take away the people's rice loaded in their huge flat bottomed boats[18].

Storage facilities were not just used to exploit changing prices over time. Merchants also needed places to store their stock when travelling to distant locations. This provided another opportunity for entrepreneurs to start a profitable business. In the large cities, storage firms appeared that were known as 'go-downs'. A book published in 1235 entitled *Splendours of the Capital* described the go-downs that existed in Hangzhou:

Within the northern water gate of the city there is a stream . . .
Along its banks, rich families have constructed several tens of
go-downs, each of which contains over a thousand units of
space, or at least several hundreds. They are used for the storage
of goods belonging to the shops in the capital and to itinerant
merchants. They are surrounded on all four sides by water, and
can so avoid being set alight by the wind (blowing flames from
other fires). Besides resisting the depredations of robbers[19].

Further information on their management is provided by the
following description:

Month by month those who have established these go-downs
demand from those who have leased space from them a sum
of cash or paper money to meet the costs of administering and
guarding the premises. They hire and maintain men to go
round on patrols at night, so that there is no laxness in the
precautions taken[20].

Market Power

Another way of maximising profit was to manipulate prices. To do
this, merchants used strategies that increased their market power.
The best way to do this was to obtain a government monopoly, but
these commonly came with price restrictions. An alternative was to
form a network with other merchants to enhance competitive
power[21]. This had the added benefit of providing security against
crime and robberies. However, government regulations often
prohibited excessive prices and profiteering, with hefty punishments
for those doing so.

Another way that a merchant could enhance profit is by deception. For example, the merchant manual *Essential Business* advises

tradesmen 'to weigh his customers silver a little lighter and his own a little heavier'[22]. However, this manual is unique in giving such advice. Most advised merchants to act fairly and with transparency. A merchant might gain from cheating his customer once, but the customer would soon discover this and would not return. He would lose his future custom. Deception was a short-sighted strategy, whereas an honest merchant would gain the same positive reputational affects that modern marketers try to create when branding.

There were other ways in which a merchant could achieve better prices, and it need not include deception. It might simply be a case of better negotiation skills. For example, a passage from the *Chen-Chiang Gazetter* (1330–2) described how:

> At the appropriate season people exchange what they have for what they have not, raising or lowering their prices in accordance with their estimation of the eagerness or lack of enthusiasm shown by others, so as to obtain the last small measure of profit[23].

A more common way by which merchants built wealth was not by making a large profit on each transaction, but to make a small profit on a large number of transactions. This approach was consistent with a Confucian view of business which favoured low prices and a more equitable distribution of resources. This did not preclude the chance to make a big profit. Writing in the year 1040, Ou-Yang Hsiu described how merchants amassed fortunes this way:

> How can the means by which a great merchant is able to amass his fortune consist of personally selling in trifling amounts in the market? He has to have peddlers and lesser merchants among whom he shares out this task. Peddlers and

lesser merchants will work not for a profit but only for a livelihood. Therefore the great merchant does not resent the
sharing in his profit, since he relies on them to market his
goods. Even if his takings are small (on each item), if his
merchandise circulates rapidly the small (profits) will mount
up to a great deal[24].

This quotation also raises the fact that, in a market economy, a
merchant is dependent on others along the supply chain. If a
merchant was too selfish and repressed others in that chain, he ran
the risk of destroying the lifeline on which his business existed.

Opportunities Along the Supply Chain

A merchant could only carry his goods to a different region if a
transportation network existed. That is why the transportation
improvements during the Tang and Song dynasties were so important. The transport links created business opportunities that otherwise would not exist. As a consequence, a number of supply-chain
options opened up by which produce might be purchased and
transported to consumers many miles away. This could be seen in
the rice market, as seen in figure 3.1[25].

The options shown in figure 3.1 reveal that business could occur
at a number of different levels. At the most basic level, business was
conducted by the peasant farmer who carried his goods to market on
his back. Their rice and that of other farmers might be bought by
wealthy villagers and landlords who stored the rice and released it on
to the market over time. At a higher level, the rice might be bought
by rice boat-merchants who would transport it to a distant market
where they could obtain a higher price. In the distant market, they
would commonly sell their stock to brokers, who would either sell to
shop-owners or alternatively sell through their own rice shops.

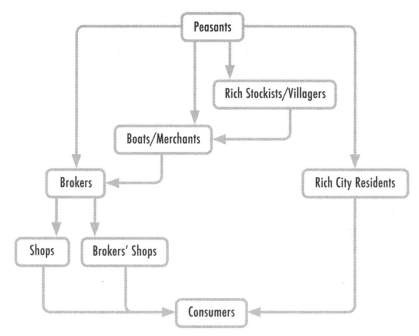

Figure 3.1   Supply-Chain Options for the Rice Market

Brokers were a particularly important part of the supply chain as they had knowledge of market conditions in distant markets. They brought buyers and sellers together, facilitating market transactions. Their knowledge of the market and the main players reduced many of the dangers that existed in the market. This could be seen in the transport industry. In the early days, a vendor would arrange the transport of their own goods but, as the market expanded, there grew a gap for specialists who could bring new players into the market, link buyers and sellers, and reduce the risks associated with transportation. Brokers filled this role:

When one is hiring a ship it is necessary to entrust a broker with the task of determining whether or not the other party is to be trusted. On all accounts you should avoid hiring on your own in the hope of so gaining some small profit. Even the old criminals and big rogues of the rivers and lakes still have difficulty in escaping the boatsmen's wiles. How much more is this the case for honest persons![26]

In using a broker, a carrier could be certain of the safe arrival of their cargoes (and passengers) at their destination[27]. In an attempt to regulate the market and provide greater confidence in it, the Song government began licensing brokers, a practice that was continued in later dynasties. Someone wanting to be a broker paid a fee to the government in return for a licence and an expectation that he would act with honesty and integrity. However, brokers could vary in their level of integrity, and later merchant manuals gave advice on how to select a broker for the first time[28].

A broker could engage in a number of activities including organising transport, storing goods and facilitating transactions between buyers and sellers. The extent to which a broker specialised depended upon the structure and size of the market in which they operated. A broker operating in a larger market could specialise in one activity and gain a competitive edge from his specialised knowledge. However, a broker operating in a small market would have limited income if they specialised too narrowly. In which case, he would need to supplement his revenue with business activities which complemented his work as a broker. He might run a hostel to house travelling merchants, provide weights and measurement facilities, tax payment facilities and possibly a shop to sell the goods in which he dealt.

Brokers were not the only ones to diversify. The owners of the inns in which travelling merchants stayed might also offer stockpiling and storage facilities to their guests. Such activities were natural additions to their existing business. The contact with their guests would indicate to them the size of the market for these facilities, thereby reducing the risk of investing in them.

ORGANISATION AND LEGAL MATTERS

Market activity occurred at a number of levels. At its most basic level, it involved a peasant taking his surplus products to market. A person used his own resources and managed his own affairs, but as the economy developed, the techniques and methods of business became more sophisticated. One of the biggest problems for small players was raising capital. A common solution to this was to seek funding from richer people either as a loan or as capital investment. By the Song dynasty, passive investment had become common. The Song author Lien Hsuan stated that 'It is general practice for the rich to entrust their money to others, to calculate the profit gained therefrom and to take half of the sum, a practice known as "putting ones money to use" '[29].

The example below from the Song dynasty illustrates how the wealthy Mr P'ei put 'his money to use' by entrusting it to a commercial manager to manage and invest:

Shen Shih-Meng from Tsao-yang (in Hupeh) had a reputation as a manager of commercial affairs throughout Kiangnan, Hunan and Hupeh. The wealthy Mr. P'ei sought and obtained his services, making him extremely welcome and interesting him with a capital of 100,000 strings of cash with which he was allowed to do as he liked. Within three years, Shen had doubled this sum, and gave the profit to his employer. He then further increased the total to 300,000 strings of cash. When old Mr P'ei died a few years later, Shen went to Lin-an to mourn him and as before to return the funds. P'ei's sons gave him thirty percent of it, which amounted to 20,000 ounces of silver[30].

This represented a significant change in the way that business was conducted. It saw the arrival of a business form in which the person who owned and invested in the business might not be the entrepreneur who managed it. The separation between ownership and management could be seen in a number of new business structures used at the time including joint ventures, partnerships and commercial networks.

Such an organisational structure involves a great deal of trust, and at times that relationship could break down, as illustrated by the case below. This was brought to a magistrate in the thirteenth century. It included one party providing credit to a man who had previously been his tutor/secretary, a relationship that enabled them to build trust. The credit enabled the tutor, Li Jun-Tsu, to get into business. While the two men initially had an amicable relationship, the same cannot be said of their wives:

I have examined the county magistrate's records concerning this matter . . . According to the deposition made by Li Jun-tsu, he opened a small rice shop in premises rented from Fan Ya.

Towards the end of 1235 Fan Ya gave him on credit some 50 piculs of rice to sell, and they made a verbal agreement that the price to be paid for these would be 50 strings of cash. In the third month of the following year, the period of the loan was extended and interest added and he was compelled to write a note of hand for 170 strings of cash . . .

According to Li Jun-Tsu's testimony, he had served as a tutor (or secretary) in Fan Ya's house for three years . . . Discord had arisen between them only because the two women of the two families had had some slight disagreement, and because when he himself had gone to Hsiao-hu to pay his respects to his parents, a crowd of Fan Ya's concubines had shamefully abused his wife Ch'en so that she had been obliged to leave – isn't this ridiculous!

Now the note of hand written by Li Jun-tsu and produced by Fan Ya says 'From the first month of 1236, a further extension. A further 3 strings of cash are to be added to the 168 strings'.

Moreover Li Jun-Tsu's deposition states that in (the years) 1228, 1229 and 1231, he was resident in Fan Ya's household as a tutor (or secretary) and that in 1234 he leased premises from Fan Ya in which to open a rice shop. Now that he was a tutor (or secretary) for up to three years is evidence of the depth of their mutual obligation. It was on account of this that Li Jun-tsu could suggest that Fan Ya lend him a little money as the capital needed to start the shop, and that Fan Ya could not refuse him. After Fan Ya had made the loan he became apprehensive that if the money were lent for a long period it might not be returned. So in 1236, he demanded a contract and Li Jun-tsu made out a note of hand for 171 strings of cash[31].

The magistrate ruled that Li Jun-Tsu was required to pay the money back, but not all of it. This case is of interest to us for a number of reasons. First, it illustrates how a person of limited resources might acquire capital to start or expand a business. People with wealth wanted to put their money to work, and entrepreneurs such as Li Jun-Tsu were ideal vehicles to do so. However, it relied on trust.

The second aspect of the court case is that the legal system would intervene in commercial disputes. It is commonly believed that the legal system in China was inadequate, and for that reason, merchants preferred to do business based on strong relationships with people they trusted. While it is true that China's legal system did not support commerce to the level found in the West, it was not absent. Nevertheless, legal battles were something a businessman would try to avoid, and maintaining a good relationship helped reduce the chance of this occurring. It was better not to get into trouble in the first place. Consequently, a merchant needed to develop skills in identifying criminal activity and the integrity of those with whom they dealt.

Contracts were recognised by Chinese courts. In fact, prototypes of contracts were in use as far back as the Han dynasty. They were commonly used for recording land transactions. Such documents specified the size and location of the land, its price and any legal responsibilities attached to the sale. The contracts also recorded the names of the buyer, seller and witnesses, as well as the scribe who was hired to write the contract. Importantly, the courts recognised these documents as evidence of legal ownership[32].

The existence of commercial contracts in the Song dynasty reflected the greater complexity of business. As goods were transported longer distances, merchants became part of very long supply chains and this increased their dependence on transporters and distributers in other regions. An example of a contract commonly used in transportation can be seen in figure 3.2 below[33].

The level of legal protection in China must not be overstated. A Confucian society was status-based and people were not equal in the eyes of the law. Secondly, the application of laws could change with circumstances. Laws could be applied with high levels of flexibility, or even discarded if the situation dictated, and this could leave a merchant without any means of legal redress. This denied Chinese business the level of certainty and security that Westerners would later enjoy.

Merchants had to buttress their limited legal protection with relationship-building strategies. In Chinese society, trust and credibility is usually confined to the inner circle of friends and family. Openness between people varies depending on the distance of social relations, and Chinese do not trust anyone who is neither friend nor family[34]. Strangers have little credibility, yet business expansion involved transactions between larger circles of people.

The increased use of brokers and contracts reflected the increased level of specialisation in the economy. As the market expanded, people could focus on one part of the market and still make a good living.

Fig 3.2   Shipping contract from the Yuan dynasty

Shipmaster . . . . . . of . . . . . in . . . . . . county in . . . . . . prefecture.

The foregoing . . . . . . , having now been guaranteed by shipping
broker . . . . . . of . . . . . . canton in . . . . . . district, undertakes to
convey . . . . . . piculs of baggage belonging to official . . . . . .
of . . . . . ., and to proceed to . . . . . . Where it will be unloaded.
As a result of the discussions between the three parties, it has
been decided that paper money worth . . . . . . strings of cash will
be paid for the hire of the boatmen, of which . . . . . . strings are
to be paid as deposit and the remainder to be handed over in full
after arrival at the destination and unloading. Once the goods
have been loaded they must be looked after carefully and (the
boatmen) shall not dare to let them get wet either through seep-
age from above or leakage from below. If they are damaged, then
restitution of like for like shall be willingly made without recourse
to the law courts. A respectfully made contract.

. . . . . . year . . . . . . month . . . . . . day.
   Shipmaster . . . . . . seal . . . . . .
   Shipping broker . . . . . . seal . . . . . .

Whether it be in farming, retail, brokering or transportation, specialisation enabled a person to further their proficiency in that area, increasing quality at the same time as reducing costs and mistakes.

Specialisation also meant that businesses became dependent on others who had the skills they lacked. Consequently, success in business required relationships with other specialists, hence a most important skill was managing relationships and choosing business partners wisely. It would be tempting for a person to avoid specialisation and therefore reduce their reliance on other people, but the person who tried to do everything himself could not compete with the network of experts that existed, as the following statement suggests:

There was a rich man in a certain place. He owned ten thousand ch'ing of agricultural land and his goods filled 1000 ships. He grew rich not by his own activities but by making use of others to act for him. One day someone said to him 'you have understood, Sir, how to amass wealth, but you do not know how to utilize it. Your ten thousand ch'ing of land bring in a mere five thousand (strings of cash) each year; your 1000 ships of goods a mere five hundred (strings of cash). This means that you, as the owner, are not getting all the profits because you share them with outsiders.

The rich man forthwith personally took over the farming of all his fields and the trading engaged in by his boats. Within three years he was poverty stricken. Why was it that, formerly, he had shared and yet been wealthy, and, latterly, had kept everything to himself and yet become poor? . . . This is simply because people exchange with each other and merchants exchange with merchants[35].

In the Tang and Song dynasties, the art of business became more sophisticated, with new ways of raising money, new business structures and new forms of commercial relationships. But if a merchant could master these activities, they could raise capital, build relationships and distribute goods in a profitable manner. The merchant would grow in wealth, while customers throughout China were provided with new products and services that could enhance the quality of their lives.

CHAPTER 4

International Trade: Southern Song to Early Ming

Chinese merchants had engaged in international business since ancient times. Probably the most famous form of international trade associated with China is the Silk Road, an ancient network of trade routes in central Asia. The most famous story linked to the opening of the Silk Road is that of Zhang Qian, a Chinese imperial envoy who was sent on a diplomatic mission around 138 BC to find allies to help fight against the Xiongnu, a nomadic people who lived on an important leg of the road.

The start of Zhang Qian's trip was a disaster. He was actually captured by the Xiongnu and held prisoner for some years, before he managed to escape and continue his journey west. He made his way to Bactria (modern-day Afghanistan) where he gained knowledge of the products that could be traded including Persian glass, silver and goldware, and horses. He returned to China[1], but twenty years later, he made a second journey. This trip was not a diplomatic mission. With knowledge of the products available and the geography of the Silk Road, he became a trader carrying large quantities of gold and silk, which he exchanged for horses[2].

This trade received a boost around 121 BC when the Chinese Han dynasty fought and defeated the Xiongnu, adding the Hexi corridor to their territory. This facilitated an increase in trade with the West which grew as the Chinese aristocracy realised an appetite for foreign sports, music, wine, dancing girls and other exotic items[3].

The Silk Road has often been portrayed as a barren pathway linking Eastern and Western civilisations, but in reality it is populated with a number of cultures. These cultures were a vital part of Silk Road trade as they were home to the markets along the route. Merchants would normally travel to a market, exchange their goods and return home. The goods might then be traded along the road, but the merchant wouldn't travel with them. It was highly unusual for a trader to start at China and walk the full length of the route to the West, or vice versa.

The routes of the Silk Road were not the only overland trade connections. Other routes connected China south with Tibet and upper Burma, and north to Mongolia and Manchuria. The markets to the north and west were particularly important sources of horses for the government which traded 'several hundred thousand' lengths of silk each year to gain them[4].

Foreigners from these distant lands also came to China to trade at the country's border markets. These markets were more like annual horse fairs than ongoing markets; nevertheless, they were still governed by strict rules. Notably, the regulations tried to keep foreigners away from local Chinese stating 'the common people must not be allowed to have intercourse with them'[5]. Each market was controlled by a high-ranking official who directed the market with the assistance of two low-ranking officials, two storekeepers, four scribes, four specialist price-fixers and eight bookkeepers. It was their responsibility to ensure that trade occurred in a fair and orderly fashion. The *Statutes on Markets and Customs Stations* states:

> Whenever there is to be a 'Market with Foreigners' with the outer barbarians or people on the borders, the officials in charge of the market should make careful inspection. A ditch should be dug around all four sides of the market place, and wattle fences (or temporary buildings) erected. Men should be posted to guard the entrances, and on the day designated for

the market, from the *mao* hour (5–7am) onwards each shall carry his goods or lead his beasts, and go to the market place. The officials shall first fix prices for the commodities with the foreigners, and only after this is done may trade begin[6].

For the Silk Road to function, it required peace and stability among the cultures that made up its length. Wars, banditry and political upheaval could end trade for long periods of time. Hence, when the Mongols established their empire across the Eurasian continent, they provided a huge impetus for international commerce. The Mongolian armies eliminated the internal wars and banditry.

The Mongol empire was established by Temujin, Genghis Khan (1162–1227), who in 1206 defeated his most powerful regional rivals and established himself as ruler of all the Mongols. He then created a powerful civil and military structure which he used to expand his power. He succeeded in conquering all the nomadic people up to the border with Persia. He reached Hungary in the west, Korea in the east and Vietnam in the south and, in 1272, his grandson Kublai Khan announced that the Mongols now ruled China, establishing the Yuan dynasty.

It was the greatest land empire in history, covering an area roughly the same size as Africa. To maintain communication in such a vast empire, the Mongols established a horse relay postal system, linked by a series of post stations, each post a day's journey apart (25–30 miles)[7]. Not only did this facilitate communication, but also security of travel as Mongol troops guarded the network[8]. Under a new 'Pax Mongolica' it became safe to travel, and trade increased as never before. Merchants from Persia, Sogdia and Central Asia all prospered as horse and camel caravans carried merchandise along the road.

The first European to travel the full length of the route was not a merchant, but a Franciscan monk, John of Plano Carpini. He was sent by Pope Innocent IV in 1245 to visit the Great Khan of Mongolia. The Khan's armies had recently threatened Europe so the Pope wanted to know his intentions. The Europeans hoped he might become an ally in the fight against Islam. The next European visitor was another Franciscan, William of Rubrouk, who met the Great Khan in 1254.

The first European merchants to cross the Silk Road included the brothers Niccolo and Maffeo Polo who met Khublai Khan in 1266, but it was Niccolo's son who became the most famous. On their second trip to China, they brought with them the seventeen-year-old Marco who stayed in China for twenty-four years. The book he wrote of his journey provided Europeans with an insight into China and its economy.

Marco Polo left us in no doubt about the power of Khublai Khan whose name he translated as 'Great Lord of Lords'. In Marco's eyes this title was well deserved as the Khan was the most powerful man who had ever lived. Polo explained that 'certainly he has right to this title, for everyone should know that this Great Khan is the mightiest man, whether in respects of subjects or of territory or of treasure, who is in the world today or who has been'[9].

Marco Polo had come from Europe's leading city, Venice; a place that conducted intercontinental trade between Europe, Africa and the Middle East, but nothing he experienced prepared him for the sights of China. Of Khan-balik (Beijing), China's new capital city, he noted:

You may take it for fact that more precious and costly wares are imported into Khan-balik than into any other city in the world. Let me give you particulars. All the treasures that come from India – precious stones, pearls and other rarities – are brought here. So too are the choicest and costliest products of Cathay itself and every other province. This is on account of

the Great Khan himself who lives here and of the lords and
ladies and the enormous multitude of hotel-keepers and other
residents and of visitors who hold the court of the Khan. That
is why the volume and value of the imports and of the internal
trade exceed those of any other city in the world[10].

He described the Grand Canal, which was a vital artery for
Chinese commerce and trade, saying:

The Great Khan ... has made a huge canal of great width
and depth from river to river and from lake to lake, and made
the water flow along it so that it looks like a big river. It
affords passage for very large ships. By this means, it is
possible to go from Manzi as far as Khan-balik[11] (southern
China to Beijing).

He also noted the role of the Yangtze River in trade, and the
importance of the salt trade which will be discussed in chapter five:

There are so many cities on its banks that, truth to tell, in the
amount of shipping it carries and the total volume and value
of its traffic, it exceeds all the rivers of the Christians put
together and their seas into the bargain ... I assure you that
the river flows through more than sixteen provinces, and
there are on its banks more than 200 cities ... This excludes
the cities and territories situated on the rivers flowing into the
main stream, which also carry much shipping ... The chief
article of commerce on this river is salt, which traders load at
this city and carry throughout all the regions lying on the
river and also up-country away from the mainstream along
the tributaries, supplying all the regions through which they
flow[12].

THE MARITIME SILK ROAD

The Silk Road was not the only trade route to the West. Merchants could also travel by ocean on what is sometimes referred to as the 'Maritime Silk Road'. The earliest seafarers to dominate this trade were not Chinese, but foreigners who had superior capabilities in ocean-going shipping. Traders from South East Asia, India and the Persian Gulf arrived in Chinese ports with goods to trade.

The Tang dynasty recognised the importance of this trade and, in the eighth century, established an office of the Commissioner for Overseas Trade. The commissioner acted as customs officer, tax collector, and purchased goods required by the government and imperial household[13]. The earliest centres of trade included Guangzhou (Canton) in the south and Yangzhou on the junction of the Grand Canal and the Yangtze River. In these towns, foreign merchants lived in officially recognised quarters establishing their own communities with their own leaders, community centres, markets, and places of worship[14].

Over time, the Chinese developed their own ocean-going capabilities. This development occurred through a number of ways. It included some level of imitation of the Arabs and Indians who dominated the trade, particularly in the area of navigation[15]. In some cases they borrowed ideas from others then improved upon them, such as the lug sail which they adapted from the Indonesians. This innovation enabled them to travel in a greater variety of wind conditions.

They also advanced ship technology and, by the tenth and eleventh centuries, had developed the seagoing junk in which they could conduct trans-oceanic trade[16]. The most impressive quality of these ships was their size. Medium-sized merchant junks from Fujian carried a cargo of approximately 120 tons and a crew of sixty,[17] while their largest ships could carry 300 tons (5,000 piculs) of cargo and 500 to 600 persons[18].

The formation of any industry is a consequence of the opportunities and constraints in the business environment, and this industry was riskier than most. All trade has its inherent risks but this one had the added risks of pirates, storms and other unfavourable ocean conditions. A ship lost at sea could lead to financial ruin. However, the Chinese environment was exceptionally favourable to the development of a maritime shipping industry. The high level of sophistication in the Chinese economy provided a number of sources of competitive advantage for the ocean-going merchant. A significant advantage came from the quality of Chinese manufacturing industries which provided marketable cargoes. Trade was conducted on the basis of barter under which the Chinese gained a strong advantage from the technological superiority of their goods. This superiority gave merchants confidence to invest in shipping as they knew their products were high in demand in offshore markets. Two of the most important were silk and ceramics.

Ceramics was another industry in which China led the world. The Chinese industry was blessed by geographic good fortune which meant that porcelain clays were highly accessible. Large quantities of Chinese glazed-ware were exported to South East Asia as early as the ninth century where their clients bought the ceramics for culinary and ritual purposes[19]. As the trade grew, Chinese merchants brought back more information on what shapes were demanded in the foreign markets, and their manufacturers responded by altering their production to make products that specifically met the cultural and consumption needs in the export markets[20].

The shipping industry also benefitted from the high levels of education and knowledge that existed throughout the economy. Taoist monks sought greater understanding of the cosmos and their experiments had created two vital inventions that reduced the cost and risk of shipping. First was gunpowder which could help merchants defend their ships from pirates. The second was the magnetic compass that was originally developed for Feng Shui (the art of siting buildings in harmony with the environment and cosmic forces). The compass revolutionised navigation and the economics of seafaring.

The official education system was another important source of knowledge. In particular, official astronomers had developed a significant body of knowledge on the night sky so that they could read the stars and foresee future events. While we might see astrology as a false science, the knowledge they gained of star movements was particularly valuable for shippers who relied on the stars for navigation.

As the shipping industry grew, jobs became more specialised with individuals advancing their capabilities and the quality of their output. The following account, although written in 1618, gives an insight into the degree of specialisation and division of labour on board the ships:

In each junk, command is in the hands of a Junk Master (po-chu). The merchants are all his dependents, like ants who have appointed a leader and move together from one nest to another. In subordinate positions are the Accountant (ts'ia-fu), who is responsible for the financial records, and the General Manager (tsung-kuan), who controls affairs on board and transmits orders on behalf of the Junk Master. There is an Arsenal Comptroller (chih-k'u) in charge of military weapons, Mast Watch Mates (a-pan) in charge of the masts, a first and Second Anchor-man ... in charge of anchors, a First and Second Sail-rope Mate ... in charge of the sail ropes, and two Helmsmen (t'o-kung) who take charge of the helm in alternation. A Chief Mate (huo-chang) watches over the compass needle, and when the route lies across a wide expanse of ocean, all obey his indications[21].

Specialisation also improved quality and reduced costs for the industry on-shore. Specialist managerial agents came into being who could be hired by wealthy merchants to conduct their maritime trade under a contract for carriage. There was a rise in the practice of hiring and chartering ships and crews, and labour hirers arose to provide men to unload sacks. Others provided carriers and porters.

The linchpins of the shipping industry were the brokers who greatly reduced transaction costs while raising the level of efficiency. A number of brokers would be located in every port acting as intermediaries between customers and transporters. They found cargoes for ships leaving port and had warehouse facilities to store goods waiting to be sold. They were extremely valuable to captains of junks who, when arriving at a port, would not necessarily be familiar with local market conditions and customs formalities. Entrusting the cargo to a broker enabled the captains to set sail after only a short time in port and spend more time in the business of carriage.

Brokers were not just of use to sea captains. They were also of value to merchants seeking transport, as merchants were not always conversant with the intricacies of shipping or aware of the abilities and reputations of captains and crews. Brokers were legally responsible for making good any losses suffered by a merchant who hired a ship[22] and this would have contributed to the maintenance of high standards. As a consequence of their function, the shipping industry became more efficient and flexible, and somewhere for investors to place their resources more confidently.

Another important position in this trade was that of the agent. Offshore agents performed an important role in reducing costs and maximising profit. In particular, they smoothed out the market fluctuations that naturally came with ocean-going trade. When a ship arrived in a foreign country with a full cargo, it ran the risk of saturating the market with the goods it carried, dramatically decreasing the prices for the goods it sold. A company could avoid this problem by employing an agent to store goods in a warehouse and release stock gradually over time, once the ship has gone, thereby gaining a higher price.

Agents also reduced the costs of buying stock. Without an agent, a ship would need to buy stock during the short time that it was in port. This could have a dramatic effect on local demand, pushing up the prices for those goods. Worse still, they might find there was insufficient supply to fill the hulls. A business that used agents overcame this problem. An agent could buy stock before the ship arrived, at lower prices, and ensure that the ship was carrying a full, cost-effective cargo.

With the use of agents, Chinese merchants were moving from free markets to organised markets, the cost of additional organisation being justified by the lower costs and higher prices it achieved. Agents also performed a key role in providing information on market conditions in foreign ports. Communication provided by the agent indicated what types of goods should be brought to the port and what sort of prices could be expected.

Most shipping was conducted by family firms headed by a male patriarch who made most of the major decisions in conjunction with other older family members. A key problem with any business is governance and trust, that is controlling the activities of staff so they act consistently with the goals of the business. It was a particular problem for international trade when agents might be away for years on end. Extended family members made ideal choices when it came to placing an agent at an offshore location. Family ties imbued staff with identity, loyalty and commitment.

Family size could limit the extent to which a family business could grow, but merchants increasingly learned to work with other companies for their mutual benefit. A commonly used option was for businesses to form networks. In such cases, each business would retain its independence but operate under the umbrella of joint concerns to enhance their competitive power and to provide protection against shipwrecks and robbery.

Partnerships also became common in which groups of merchants shared the ownership of ships and goods. A merchant entering such an agreement must be able to trust his partner, so strongly considered their partner's reputation before acting. Seen in this light, reputation became a valuable business asset that enhanced a business's commercial options and opportunities. Consequently, a businessman strove to build and maintain a reputation for being capable and trustworthy as part of his business practice.

Some partnerships might only last for one voyage, after which the partners shared their profits. Other partnerships were more permanent and covered a number of voyages, however, the scope of these partnerships was clearly limited to the skills and resources that each partner brought. Other new organisational forms that made it easier to raise capital were the commenda and commercial money-lending. The commenda is a structure in which a wealthy person or merchant entrusted money or goods to another merchant who makes use of the capital, and shares out the profits at the end.

The rise of these activities reveals increasing instances where the ownership of ships and capital became separated from their management. This further complicates the problem of governance. One concept from Confucianism that underlied commercial relationships is reciprocity, that is, giving in the expectation that sooner or later you will receive something in return[23]. This leads to the development of obligation and trust.

The other concept that encouraged businessmen to be honest was the notion of 'losing face' (reputation). Relationship contracting of this kind works best when parties realise they are bound to a repeating activity, that is, they must work again with that person in the future. In which case, a businessman would be foolish to try to exploit those with whom he dealt. The potential for future business means it is in no one's interest to engage in exploitive behaviour[24].

The levels of profit earned by these traders could be immense.

For example a merchant by the name of Cai Jingfang earned a net profit of 980,000 strings of cash on his trade through Quanzhou for the period 1127–34, an average of 122,500 strings per year[25]. To place this in perspective, an ordinary soldier earned an annual salary of between fifty and seventy strings of cash[26]. Marco Polo gives insight into the breakdown of the costs and profit of ocean-going ships:

> ... all the ships coming from India pay a 10 per cent duty on all their wares ... Payment for the hire of ships, that is for freight, is reckoned at the rate of 30 per cent on small wares, 44 per cent on pepper and 40 per cent on aloes and sandalwood, and all bulky wares. So that, what with freight and imperial tithe, the merchants pay half the value of what they import[27].

After these expenses were paid, merchants made 'such a profit that they ask nothing better than to return with another cargo'. With merchants willing to reinvest these large profits, shipping fleets could reach substantial size. One ship owner had a fleet of eighty ships and clearly had to use a managerial agent or hire ships out[28]. However, most investors preferred not to concentrate their investments, but, to diversify and spread them. This helped them overcome 'hazards of both a natural and a social kind'. This meant not just the risks of storms and wrecks, but antagonistic government officials and a society that still did not fully welcome the seeking of profit. Merchants would endeavour to conceal their investments through the use of others. Land was perennially regarded as the safest place to invest wealth.

Fujian and Ibn Battuta

> The entire province of Fujian makes its living by the practice of seaborne commerce[29].
>
> (Observation by a Song dynasty scholar)

In the Tang dynasty, the leading centre for ocean trade was the port of Guangzhou (Canton) which received the vast majority of foreign merchants. However, in the following centuries, nearby Fujian took the lead. Fujian's initial rise occurred when the Tang dynasty fell in 907. The province experienced a period of independence and could now be governed with its own interests coming first, not those of China[30]. The province's independent rulers encouraged maritime trade, and the development of Quanzhou as the leading port which began to build its own communities of foreign merchants. The visible evidence of this could be seen in the construction of mosques: a clear indication that Muslim merchants were coming to the town.

This development continued during the Song dynasty (960–1276) which reunified China. The Song dynasty continued to recognise the contribution that commerce could make to government revenue. This income was particularly important given the continual threat that northern armies were posing China. The money was needed to fund the army. In 1127, Jurchin invaders from the north defeated the Chinese army and occupied northern China. They captured the capital city of Kaifeng which had previously been the economic engine for the country. The Jurchin invasion put an end to Kaifeng's predominance and the Song court was forced to flee south of the Yangtze River where they established a new capital at Hangzhou. From this point on, the dynasty is known as the Southern Song dynasty.

With a much smaller economy to manage, the government became more reliant on income from commerce, so encouraged international trade. This positive atmosphere enabled Fujian merchants to develop their maritime skills in relative freedom. The officials taxed the merchants but otherwise left them alone to conduct business as they saw fit[31]. Encouraged by the government, family firms invested in ocean-going ships and their cargos. Early ventures that returned healthy profits encouraged others to make similar investments. In this environment, Fujian shippers developed their maritime skills, while traders gained experience of international markets.

Fujian ships left China each year, following the opportunities that the monsoon winds provided. They often left agents in foreign ports, and in this way China developed its own communities of offshore merchants. Communities of Fujian traders (and some from Guangdong) emerged in the major ports of Champa, Cambodia, Sumatra and Java[32]. Some of them settled down, married local women, and produced children who traded with their cousins back in China over the next generation.

Through this process, the Fujians emerged as China's most successful overseas traders, a position they held from the thirteenth to the eighteenth centuries[33]. Back in China, Fujian ports became the leading harbours for ocean-going shipping. By the time the Mongols established the Yuan dynasty, Quanzhou had become the largest port in the world. Marco Polo was particularly impressed when he arrived there, saying it:

> . . . is the port for all ships that arrive from India laden with costly wares and precious stones of great price and big pearls of fine quality. It is also a port for the merchants of Manzi, that is, of all the surrounding territory, so that the total amount of traffic in gems and other merchandise is a marvel to behold . . . I can tell you further that the revenue accruing to the Great Khan from this city and port is something colossal, because I would have you know that all the ships coming from India pay a 10 per cent duty on all their wares[34].

Another international traveller to visit Quanzhou was Ibn Battuta, but unlike Marco Polo who arrived overland, he took the maritime silk road. Ibn Battuta (1304–69) was a scholar and traveller from

Morocco. He travelled overland to Calicut, India, from where he took a ship and travelled the maritime road to China. Calicut was one of India's leading ports. Ibn Battuta noted that 'it gathers merchants from all quarters. Its harbour is one of the largest in the world.'[35] When he arrived, there were thirteen Chinese vessels in port waiting for the monsoon season to change and allow them to sail home. He noted that the Chinese now dominated this route: 'On the sea of China travelling is done in Chinese ships only.'[36]

In 1345, he arrived in Quanzhou and, like Marco Polo before him, was astonished by the country's wealth. He stated explicitly 'there is no people in the world wealthier than the Chinese'[37]. His observations of the Fujian port confirmed those of Marco Polo, stating, 'It's harbour is among the biggest in the world, or rather it is the biggest; I have seen about a hundred big junks there and innumerable little ones.'[38]

Fujian produced a number of manufactured goods which provided cargos for their shippers. These included copper and ceramics. These products were exported to foreign lands where they were traded for imports[39]. Ibn Battuta admired the locally produced pottery that he saw; however, he had no idea how they made it. He claimed:

> It is made from an earth from mountains there which burns like charcoal . . . they add to it a stone which is found there and burn it for three days. Then they pour water on it and it becomes powdery again. Then they ferment it . . .
>
> It is exported to India and other parts of the world till it reaches our country in the Maghrib. It is the most superb kind of pottery[40].

Ibn Battuta also witnessed the important role that the Chinese government played in the economy, and he was left with mixed impressions. He was particularly impressed with the security that China offered merchants on overland routes:

China is the safest and best country for the traveller. A man travels for nine months alone with great wealth and has nothing to fear. What is responsible for this is that in every post station in their country is a fundaq which has a director living there with a company of horse and foot. After sunset or nightfall, the director comes to the fundaq with his secretary and writes down the names of all the travellers who will pass the night there, seals it and locks the door . . . In the morning he and his secretary come and call everybody by name and write down a record. He sends someone with the travellers to conduct them to the next post station and he brings back a certificate from the director of that fundaq confirming that they have all arrived[41].

However, he was less impressed by official intervention at ocean ports like Quanzhou:

It is the custom of the Chinese that when a junk wished to set sail, the admiral and his secretaries come aboard and record the archers, servants and sailors who will sail; the junk is then free to leave. When it returns they come aboard again and compare what they recorded with the persons on the junk. If one of those recorded is missing they question the owner of the junk about him, asking for proof that he is dead, or has escaped, or whatever else it may be has happened to him. If he cannot provide this, he is arrested.

They have done that, they order the ship's master to dictate to them a manifest of all the merchandise in it, whether small or great (in value). Then everyone disembarks and the customs

officials sit to inspect what they have with them. If they come
upon any article that has been concealed from them, the junk
and whatever is in it is forfeit to the treasury. This is a kind of
extortion I have seen in no country, whether infidel or Muslim,
except China[42].

Ibn Battuta's observation of confiscation is supported by other
documents of the time[43]. This situation is made worse by the varying
integrity of officials. Lu Zhan, the trade superintendent of Quanzhou
in the first decade of the twelfth century, noted 'the clerks were
seldom pure and the merchants suffered from their pilfering'[44]. Lu
was confronted with endemic corruption among his staff when he
obtained his position.

Ibn Battuta stayed in the Islamic quarter of Quanzhou and
enjoyed the hospitality of those who shared his faith, but despite his
experience of international travel, Ibn Battuta displayed a response
that is not uncommon for international travellers today – culture
shock. He stated:

China, for all its magnificence, did not please me. I was deeply
depressed by the prevalence of infidelity in the lodgings and
when I left my lodgings I saw many offensive things which
distressed me so much that I stayed at home and went out
only when it was necessary. When I saw Muslims, it was as
though I had met my family and my relatives[45].

TRIBUTE TRADE AND ZHENG HE

The bulk of Chinese trade throughout this time was conducted by
private enterprise, but it was not the only trade. The government had
been involved in foreign trade since the Han dynasty (206 BC– AD 9).
The trade was in the hands of palace eunuchs who exchanged silks

for jewels, glass and other exotic objects[46]. The purchase of horses for the army was another item of particular importance to the government. However, this trade was not regular. In the Southern dynasties (420–589) there appears to be only one mission every one and a half years[47].

The Chinese government conducted a particular kind of international trade with its neighbours called tribute trade. It was not just an exchange of goods, but a tool of diplomacy in which the Chinese legitimised their power and supremacy. China's neighbours sent goods as a sign of submission and, in return, the Chinese government exported products as a reward for their loyalty and respect[48].

The tribute trade reached its peak in the early Ming dynasty. For example, in 1385 Korea displayed its loyalty by sending five thousand horses, twenty-five kilograms of gold, 14,000 kilograms of silver and 50,000 bolts of cotton[49]. A few years later, the kingdom of Ayutthaya (Thailand) sent more than 77,000 kilograms of aromatic wood, while a Japanese mission sent nine ships carrying over half a million kilograms of goods, including 12,000 kilograms of sulphur and 37,000 swords.

Government enterprise reached an unprecedented scale with the voyages of Admiral Zheng He. Between 1405 and 1431, the admiral led seven voyages to Java, Sumatra, Ceylon, India, Arabia and Africa. His fleet consisted of 317 ships, carrying some 28,000 men, that left China in 1405; an immense display of power designed to raise awareness of the supremacy of the Chinese emperor.

There have been some ridiculous claims made about these voyages, including statements that they may have reached America, Australia and New Zealand. These claims were popularised in a best-selling book entitled *1421*, but the book contains inadequate research. These voyages were well documented by the Chinese and we know exactly where Zheng He travelled. For example, the interpreter on the fourth, sixth and seventh voyages was a man by the name of Ma Huan who recorded an account of his mission, entitled the *Yingya Shenglan*[50]. It provides a large body of information on the sea lanes, navigation conditions and harbours of value to seamen and merchants. He describes the customs, social systems and commercial practices in ports they visited on the way to the Persian Gulf, Red Sea and east Africa. These were 'the most distant places the fleet visited'[51]. An extract below describes his visit to Malacca:

> Eight days due south by ship from Champa [part of present-day Vietnam] one arrives at Longyamen [perhaps the entrance to the strait between Bintan Island and Batam Island]. Malacca is two days west from here[52].

Of interest to merchants is his list of products from the area, including *huanglianxiang* (a perennial used as a digestive and also as a dye), *wumu* (ebony), *huaxi* (tin), and agricultural products such as sweet potatoes, bananas and *boluomi* (jack fruits, a type of bread-fruit). He states that the Malaccans used tin for the trading currency and built 'storehouses into which they put all their coins and food-stuffs. When a ship bound for other lands comes there, they take out their trading goods and load them on board.'[53]

As magnificent as Zheng He's fleets were, the benefit did not justify the cost, particularly when northern invaders were threatening Chinese borders again. The money spent on these voyages was needed for defence and the Great Wall of China. The last fleet sailed in 1431. The Chinese turned away from ocean trade, a situation made worse by the fact that the Ming dynasty was becoming anti-business. Traditional Confucian values were given priority, much to the detriment of merchants who were now banned from travelling overseas.

The activities of Chinese merchants were always dependent on the policy climate at the imperial court. Fluctuations in trading patterns reflected the extent to which Confucians held power at the court. If eunuchs held power, merchants could expect more free-dom. However, it wasn't just a case of internal politics. Merchants might be able to ignore central policy if they gained support from the officials in their local town, far away from the imperial court. Local mandarins did not always adhere to central policy and, if paid a bribe, could be quite accommodating of merchant's interests. However, financial exchange was not always necessary as some mandarins recognised the value of trade. There was much variation in thought among the Confucian scholars, and the conservatives did not always hold the ascendency. Nevertheless, the early Ming was a bad time for business, both domestic and international, as we will discover in the next chapter.

CHAPTER 5

Ming Dynasty (1368–1644)

How important to people are wealth and profit! Human disposition is such that people pursue what is profitable to them, and with this profit in mind they will even face harm. They gallop in pursuit of it day and night, never satisfied with what they have, though it wears down their spirits and exhausts them physically. Profit is what people covet.

Zhang Han, 'On Merchants'[1]

The Yuan dynasty was short-lived. In the fourteenth century, the Mongols lost control of their empire and were overthrown by ethnic Chinese who established the Ming dynasty in 1368. The first Ming emperor had to rebuild a country that had experienced many years of war, famine and natural disasters[2], and through this process of reconstruction, set out to rid China of Mongolian influences, replacing them with traditional Confucian values.

This return to Confucian values included a focus on agriculture as the basis of the economy, not commerce. Accordingly, a number of anti-market policies were introduced. The imperial court determined that the country's resources were no longer to be allocated through the market, but by government decree. The new economy was a command economy with instructions issued from the top down.

A potent illustration of the new regime could be seen in the treatment of Shen Wansen who was considered the richest man living south of the Yangtze River. Shen started his career like many other Chinese, working as a farmer for his father. He came from Zhouzhang, a well-irrigated region with a good climate for agriculture. Shen was clearly very capable and began acquiring additional land. His efforts brought him to the attention of Lu Deyuan, a man of significant wealth living in Suzhou. Lu agreed to finance Shen's activities and with this capital backing, Shen further developed his farming activities and began trading silk and tea. He eventually took these products on to the export market, while importing jewels, ivories and spices in return.

Land remained an important part of his investment portfolio. It is said that when the Yuan dynasty began to fall, he purchased land at rock-bottom prices from Mongols fleeing Ming patriots. Then, when peace returned and the land market stabilised, he sold the land at normal prices, making a fortune in the process.

However, Shen's wealth made him the target of jealousy. With the emperor hoping to create a more equal society, he targeted Shen's wealth. At first, the emperor forced Shen to pay for one third of the wall being built around the city of Nanjing. He then took over Shen's private garden. However, social equality does not apply to emperors so when Shen's furniture was confiscated, it found a new home in the emperor's palace[3]. Shen was eventually stripped of all his assets and sent to exile in Yunan.

The early Ming dynasty was not a good time for business. The policies of Emperor Zhu Yuanzhang took away many freedoms that the Chinese had previously taken for granted. To gain greater control of society, the *lijia* system was introduced. Under this system, the government registered farmers and artisans in the locations they lived, and placed families in groups of ten. Once registered, the government forbade them from moving from those locations or changing their profession. This population control also served as the basis of taxation, as restrictions on travel meant people could not escape paying tax by moving to a new location.

Aspects of the policy reflected a return to the system that existed before the Tang dynasty, and the results were devastating for commerce. The restrictions on migration, travel and employment reduced the functioning of the market economy, as merchants could no longer travel and distribute their goods.

The two principal forms of tax were a poll tax paid in grain or corvée labour in which workers had to provide labour free of charge for use by the government. The government used this free workforce to rebuild China's infrastructure, industries and public buildings. These included the building of the three capitals Nanjing, Fengyang and Beijing, and the reconstruction of the Grand Canal which had fallen into disrepair under the Mongols. With tax paid in kind or through labour, taxes were no longer paid by coins. In fact, the government prohibited the use of coins and silver throughout the economy. This demonetisation made it hard for merchants to perform transactions.

The early Ming economy shared many characteristics with the command economies that appeared in the twentieth century. Not only was the tight economic control similar to that which existed in the Soviet Union and China, but both shared a desire to have a more egalitarian society. For example, it has been argued that the organisation of families into closed communities was partly motivated by a desire to ensure egalitarian access to land[4]. The government also introduced other measures to protect the populace. For example, in the first year of his reign, the emperor ordered the construction of granaries in every county, to store grain for use in times of shortage and famine.

Despite these positive motives, it would seem that the overall effect of these policies was to reduce the welfare of the average Chinese[5]. In a command economy, resources are distributed through top-down coercion, with the average person losing significant freedoms. More importantly, with restrictions on movement, occupations and the use of money, resource distribution lacked the scope and efficiency that the market can achieve. Incomes declined across the country, while opportunities to create a business evaporated[6].

This command economy lasted for a century, but began to unravel at the end of the fifteenth century as market forces reappeared. Ironically, the government's activities helped the reformation of the market, although it was not the government's intention. One of their key projects was the reconstruction of the Grand Canal which had fallen into disuse under the Mongols. When the government repaired the canal, it increased the possibility that long-distance trade would return.

The canal needed significant resources and administration to remain open. Approximately 47,000 labourers were needed to maintain facilities, operate locks, keep levees and banks in repair, and handle the boats[7]. In the early Ming, this labour came from the corvée tax system. The grain barges using the canal were also provided by the government. By the mid-fifteenth century, 11,775 barges were operating on the canal[8]. Boatmen on the barges were permitted to carry a small, limited volume of goods which facilitated a small amount of trade. Over time, other boats began to take advantage of the restored transportation system, and producers and merchants began sending surplus products to other regions where they could make a healthy profit.

Throughout the mid to late Ming, other changes in the business environment increased the commercialisation of the economy. This included tax reforms. In 1436, the government allowed the grain-tax payment to be made in cash. A further round of taxation reforms in the 1560s, known as the 'single whip' reforms, overhauled the whole system and allowed a single tax payment[9]. An example of the change can be seen in the porcelain industry. Before the tax changes, a potter would have to provide three months of labour free to the government, every four years. After the changes, he would have to pay 0.45 liang of cash a year (at a time when a skilled potter might earn up to 12 liang a year)[10]. This represented a 40 per cent decline in their tax burden. It also had the benefit of simplifying the tax process, thereby making it easier for the government to administer.

Another effect of the tax change was to increase the use of money in the economy. In order to raise money, labourers increasingly chose to hire out their labour and be paid a cash wage. The cash they earned did not just pay their taxes, but also enabled them to buy other goods and services, thereby expanding the number of market transactions occurring in the economy. Workers also gained greater mobility to choose where they worked.

Another change that helped the commercialisation of the economy was the influx of silver into China, carried there by European traders. The first European ship arrived in 1513, captained by the Portuguese Jorge Álvares. Trade with the Portuguese grew over the sixteenth century to the point where they established a permanent base on the island of Macao, paying an annual rent of 18.9 kilograms (41.6 pounds) of silver. The Portuguese also conducted trade between China and Japan, another source of silver.

But it was the arrival of the Spanish in the Philippines that truly stimulated the influx of silver. In 1521, the Portuguese captain Ferdinand Magellan arrived in Asia; however, he was not sailing for Portugal but for Spain. He claimed the Philippine Islands for the Spanish crown and, from 1565, a process of colonisation began. At the same time, a shipping connection, the 'Manila Galleon' was formed with Spanish colonies in South America. The American colonies possessed mines with immensely wealthy mineral deposits. Silver from these mines was shipped across the Pacific Ocean to Manila where Chinese merchants traded silk, porcelains and other products for silver, which they then carried back to China.

The influx of silver had a profound effect on the Chinese economy[11]. Chinese merchants gained confidence in the value and use of money. The number of cash transactions increased, while more and more industries began to produce for the open market, including agriculture, silk and porcelain. These products spread across the country in newly created trade networks. The entrepreneurs who created these networks were helping to facilitate China's second great commercial boom; the first being during the Tang and Song dynasties.

A number of commercial groups or syndicates emerged during this time. They were comprised of merchants who came from the same geographic region and were commonly related to each other; however, the merchants who were most successful in this booming economy were those based in Huizhou. Merchants from Huizhou established themselves in all the empire's major towns and cities. Such was their pervasiveness, that a saying of the time had it that 'a place could not be considered a town if it did not have Huizhou merchants'[12].

Huizhou Merchants

The Huizhou region was characterised by valleys and infertile hills which meant that agricultural production was low and the region was reliant on imports for many of its food supplies. This forced the local population to become active in trade, as a local historian notes:

> Even in the best years, the crop yield is too low and only about one-tenth of the annual food requirement can be produced. The people engage in trade and commerce so they can obtain the other nine-tenths from elsewhere[13].

The Huizhou region was always short of grain and a number of merchants built their first businesses in this commodity. They may have started in business by obtaining supplies for their home region, but soon they were using their knowledge to sell grain in other areas. The following report describes how a Huizhou merchant made a large profit from the price differences between regions:

There was a noted family in Caishi who had built up a fleet of boats ... A merchant from Huizhou hired a boat from them to carry grain. He took it to Wumen and sold when the price was high enough. In two or three days he had sold out and made a huge profit, so he hurried back and went off to trade in Nankou[14].

With poor agricultural fertility, the region relied primarily on the export of handicrafts including ink, paper and lacquerware to pay for its imports[15]. The one agricultural product that could be grown in the region was tea, in the Qimen area. Trading in tea and handicraft products gave merchants experience in distribution which they could later apply to other commercial ventures. In this way, they had the good fortune of developing business capabilities at a time when the market economy was about to boom. They were well placed to take advantage of the opportunities that were about to be presented. By the mid-Ming dynasty, they were dealing in a large array of products including salt, rice, timber, cotton, silk, porcelain and tea, and were also involved in moneylending[16].

The profits they made through trade meant they had significant capital, which put them in a good position to buy government licences for the distribution of salt. In the Ming and Qing dynasties, salt was organised as a state monopoly. With restricted competition, the salt monopoly could provide high profits for those who had a licence. The government's Salt Administration was located close to Huizhou, at nearby Yangzhou. Many merchants moved to Yangzhou, a move which must have facilitated greater co-operation with the government.

A record of one Huizhou merchant came from the Ming writer Wang Taokun, who recorded how his forefathers made their fortunes out of salt:

Since the time of my great-grandfather, my family have been model sons who worked hard in the fields. They honoured the salt certificate system since my grandfather exalted trade. My great-grandfather stopped trading with the north and moved to Hangzhou where their business grew rapidly[17].

Huizhou's location also gave the merchants an advantage when dealing with porcelain. The region was located close to Poyang Lake, an important trade artery in the distribution of ceramics made in the town Jingdezhen. Some merchants may have even exported clay to the potters at Jingdezhen. Huizhou merchants became active in the porcelain trade, distributing ceramic products throughout the country.

Over time, the merchants expanded their activities beyond trade as some invested in production. The process by which they became owners of industrial plants appears to be similar to the way that merchants became capitalists in the iron industry during the Song dynasty. If a porcelain manufacturer got into financial trouble, the merchants had enough capital to underwrite them and, through this process, gained significant control of the porcelain industry.

A description of one such merchant comes from Pan Cijun, whose father had operated as a licensed salt trader travelling in the area around the Yangtze and Huai rivers[18]. He also began trading in grain and cotton cloth, before moving into porcelain from Jingdezhen, as the following description relates:

He was said to have always been one step ahead of the other merchants, and just when everyone thought he was bound to lose money, would make a sudden profit. At that time, traders on the Chang river, that is at Jingdezhen, used to make their orders up with some poor quality goods, but when Pan started dealing with the town, he gave a huge banquet for local worthies at which it was agreed that this practice would stop. Then, in a particularly bad year when the potters were reduced to stealing food and fighting had broken out, Pan took over a large number of local debts and extended the periods of loan or even burnt the contracts. He also bought up all available pottery irrespective of the quality. Everyone wanted to sell to him because of his generosity so he cornered the market and when he eventually resold the goods, made a three hundred per cent profit[19].

This example is notable for two points. First, Pan's father recognised the importance of quality if he was to receive a high price for the product. Second, he engaged in the age-old practice of cornering the market. Chinese merchants were very aware of the importance of market power to raise profits. Normally, market power was acquired through the government limiting entry such as with the salt monopoly, but in this instance it was achieved by buying up all the supply. This strategy can only be used by someone with access to sufficient capital to buy all the product supplied.

The Huizhou merchants, like other merchant groups of the time, operated as extended family networks. Young men from the district began their careers working in the businesses of their fathers, uncles or cousins, where they served an apprenticeship. Their base might be in their hometown where they kept their families, but the men would spread out across the country building networks along which they moved their products. This might involve significant travel and many years away from home[20].

A merchant was always conscious of the negative stigma associated with being in business so might not want all his sons to follow him into trade. Consequently, on gaining success a businessman would buy official positions, invest in land and finance his children's education in the hope that they would become scholar-officials. Such acts also facilitated closer connections with government. In this age of economic transformation, it was not uncommon for a wealthy commercial family to metamorphose into a merchant-scholar-official family within two or three generations[21]. An example of an individual who became an official on the basis of his family's wealth was Zhang Han. In the passage below, he describes how his family became wealthy.

Ancestor Yian was of a humble family and made liquor as his profession. In the closing years of Chenghua (1465–1487) there was a flood. At that time my great-grandfather was living beside a river, and when the water flooded it entered the building. All the liquor he was making was completely spoiled. For several evenings he went out to look at his spoiled liquor and inundated jugs. One evening as he was returning home, someone suddenly called him from behind. My great-grandfather turned to greet him, and was handed something warm. Suddenly the person was not to be seen.

When he got home he lit the lamp and shone it on what turned out to be a small ingot of silver. With this he gave up making liquor and bought a loom. He wove ramie (*zhu*) and silk (*bi*) of several colours, and achieved a very high level of craftsmanship. Every time a roll of fabric came off the loom, people competed to buy it. He calculated his profit at 20%. After saving for twenty years he bought another loom.

Later he increased his looms to over twenty. The merchants who dealt in textiles constantly thronged the house inside and out, and still he couldn't meet their orders. Hereafter, the family profession brought great wealth. The next four ancestors carried on the profession, each gaining wealth in the tens of thousands. The story of his receiving silver late that night is very strange, yet since the time of my great-grandfather it has been passed down. How is it that it should have started with a spirit's gift?[22]

The idea that someone would give a silver ingot to a stranger and disappear does not seem believable, and one is tempted to think that in a state of hardship caused by the floods, he stole the capital that launched his business. Whatever the source of this silver, the family invested in textiles during a time when the market was growing and provided the family with substantial returns.

This wealth enabled Zhang Han to receive a good Confucian education. On passing the provincial examinations he gained his first official posting in 1536, followed by a number of government posts before retiring in 1577. During his retirement, he wrote a number of essays including one entitled *On Merchants* which gives us insight into merchant practices at the time. His experience as an official gave him great exposure to merchant activities, as he writes, 'I have had occasion to travel on official business all over the country, and have gathered reports on the fortunes of merchants.'[23]

Zhang Han was well aware of the prosperity that commerce provided, not just for the rich, but for all members of society. And he was well aware of the social cost that would occur if it collapsed. For example, of the textile industry he stated, 'From what I have seen, if the dyeing workshops were to close down, the displaced workers would number several thousand; and if the weaving workshops were to close down, the displaced workers would number another several thousand.'[24] Consequently, he was very concerned about the state of commerce, and he became particularly vocal about the damaging effects of too much regulation and taxation. He believed that merchants were faced with excessive taxation demands:

This must be stopped. At every point where a merchant passes a customs house or a ford, the officials there either insist on unloading the carts or docking the boats and checking through the sacks and crates, or just overestimate the value and collect excessive payment. What has passed the customs house or ford has already been taxed, yet the markets then tax it again. One piece of merchandise should be subject to one taxing[25].

Zhang Han had personally reduced taxes in a region he administered, and discovered this did not reduce the total tax take. In fact, the resulting growth in business meant that more tax was paid:

I held office as Bureau Secretary in the Ministry of Works in Nanjing, and was responsible for customs duties in upper and lower Longjiang. At the time I was working together with Associate Censor Fang Keyong. I said to him: '. . . How can we let people say that in the present they lack benevolent government?' Fang agreed with me, and together we rescinded merchants' taxes by twenty percent. From this time on, merchants delighted in coming, their boats sculling in like spokes to a hub. The state tax revenue when compared with before actually increased by fifty percent. From this it can be seen that people's minds are moved by the government's benevolence[26].

Zhang noted that there were different levels of markets. At the lowest level were the periodic markets where local farmers and other producers gathered on a regular basis to exchange their goods with others. No merchants were needed in such markets as producers sold their own wares. However, this was not a process that would create great wealth, as Zhang Han notes of these 'poor traders who stick at home, completely ignorant that there is something to be gained abroad'. On the other hand, those who were prepared to travel could make significant returns:

From Anqing and Taihu to Xuancheng and Huizhou, many people have an eye for profits from speculative trading, abandoning the primary sector to pursue the secondary. They transport grain, singing as they scull, heading for the capital of former emperors and kings (Nanjing) ... The best merchants who go to market make several hundred percent profit, those second to them make a hundred percent profit, and the lowest and least talented ones still get ten percent.[27]

Those merchants who left their homes and circulated products around their county or prefecture were in a better positon to gain profits. However, the wealthiest and most powerful merchants were those who engaged in inter-regional trade[28]. They were the ones who could most exploit regional differences in supply and price. However, a travelling merchant was exposed to the vagaries of the market and the dangers of travel, and many unsuccessful merchants shamefully stayed away from home rather than admit their failure.

Salt Merchants

The official Zhang Han was emphatic on which industries provided the greatest profits, saying 'the profits on salt and tea are greatest. Those who aren't big merchants cannot take on these trades ...'[29] He continued:

Most of the wealthy from my home province of Zhejiang have built that wealth through salt, though a certain merchant surnamed Jia in Hangzhou created his wealth by selling tea and, after several generations, that wealth has not been exhausted[30].

It was no coincidence that the wealthiest merchants observed by Zhang Han were in the salt and tea trades, as these were government monopolies in which competition was limited. The salt merchants in particular were fabulously wealthy. They have been described as the 'aristocracy' of merchants and the 'unchallenged merchant princes of China'[31]. The salt merchants of Yangzhou possessed some of the largest fortunes and certainly possessed the largest capital base of any commercial and industrial group in the Chinese empire[32].

Throughout the Ming and Qing dynasties, production and distribution of salt was tightly regulated and monitored by the government. The Lianghuai region was the most important salt district with its administration based at Yangzhou, a city located close to the canals that carried the salt from the salt fields on the coast. Yangzhou was also close to two major waterways on which the salt was transported to other markets. As the location of the Salt Administration, it attracted wealthy merchants from outside the region who came to build relationships with officials and acquire salt licences. Once again, it was the Huizhou merchants who came to play a dominating role in the industry.

To understand how these merchants became so wealthy, it is necessary to understand the structure and operations of the salt industry. Production of salt began at the salterns. These were surrounded by salt ponds and fields which produced the raw brine from which salt was extracted (either by evaporation or lixiviation). The salterns were owned by a salt master (*tsao-hlu*) who also owned the salt fields attached to it. The Ming government clearly defined his activities and limitations. The idea was to create opportunities for small, stable businesses that could be passed on to the next generation. However, this model was soon undermined by the forces of capitalism.

The salterns provided salt to factories of which there were thirty at the beginning of the Qing dynasty. The factory manager would buy salt from the salterns and then take it to Yangzhou where it would be sold to transport merchants. Storage depots were built which might be jointly owned by the salt master and merchant, or might be erected by the government.

The factory merchants' original purpose was to purchase the salt from the salterns and distribute it to the transport merchants, but over time this changed, with many of them becoming owners of the salterns. The structure of production meant that the factory managers were in a strong position to reap most of the profits. The government had structured the industry so that the salterns had to sell their salt to their local factory merchant. This meant each local factory merchant had monopoly buying powers. This put him in a position to be a price maker, buying 'salt at a price more or less dictated by him'. Unsurprisingly, one study showed that 50–60 per cent of the profit went to the factory merchants, while the depots and salterns received about 20 per cent each[33].

Factory managers acquired significant capital and many ended up buying the salterns that supplied them. In some cases, a saltern might go through a tough period in which they needed a loan. On such occasions, the factory manager might forward a loan, a process by which he could obtain significant financial control, if not joint ownership of the business.

The other part of this industry was in transport and distribution. The factory managers would deliver their salt to the city of Yangzhou where the Salt Administration was based. There, the salt would be sold to a transport merchant at a mutually agreed price. Transport merchants held licences from the Salt Administration which enabled them to distribute salt to a particular location in China. They effectively gained a regional monopoly which meant there would be no competition on the route. Merchants would bid for a licence, and the successful bidders would need to pay for it in advance. Hence the system favoured those who already had capital and, at subsequent bids, those who had made money from previous licences had an advantage which excluded new entrants and smaller operators.

Transport merchants were the industry's merchant princes, and would often lease their rights to lower-level merchants who handled the daily trade. The transport or 'head' merchants would supervise the smaller merchants. Although the smaller merchants are described as 'small', in reality they were substantial merchants in their own right. Their fortunes only seemed small in comparison to the head merchants with whom they worked. The head merchants built some of the largest fortunes the world had seen at the time, a comparison which would make any merchant seem small.

The small merchants would normally trade under the name of the head merchant, who not only represented them in dealings with the government but also covered any tax arrears incurred by the small merchants. This model of having a head merchant representing a small group is one that we will find again in Chinese business (among the Co-Hong in chapter 8 and Chinese living overseas in chapter 9).

The transportation side of the industry was initially structured so as to favour small merchants, but, as with the production side, the industry became concentrated with the trade being dominated by a few powerful families with strong government connections. Over time, the small group of head merchants became a ruling elite, fabulously wealthy with accusations of scandalous behaviour. Their close relationships with the officials at the Salt Administration enabled them to reap a large portion of the salt trade. In return, the officials received generous gifts and entertainment.

At a time when 60,000 taels was considered a sizeable fortune, it is estimated that head merchants had fortunes of up to 10 million taels. In China, a merchant selling 10,000 taels of goods a year would be considered a large capitalist merchant; however, a salt merchant could earn 300,000 taels in one year from the salt business, and they often had investments in other industries to augment this[34].

The disparities in income did not remain unnoticed by government officials. For example, the official Han Wen noted how small merchants were being 'pushed out of the market by the merchants working for powerful families'[35]. Han Wen believed that corruption and ill-practice was occurring at a number of levels in the industry. For example, he claimed that agents acting for the powerful merchants would receive more salt from the salt factories than their licences allowed, but local officials were too scared to take action because of the power and connections that the merchants held[36].

Some Ming officials traced problems with the salt monopoly to the system under which it operated. Weaknesses in the rules and procedures meant that dishonest individuals could exploit the system to increase profit. Many of these problems also occurred in the tea monopoly. One official who wrote on the tea administration was Jiang Bao. He believed that 'miscreant merchants' were able to smuggle tea because 'of the greed of local officials who did not fear the law and actively participated in and tolerated' unauthorised commerce[37]. He believed that an illegal salt trade was developing outside the official system. This occurred because of collusion between the merchants and local officials who were meant to be repressing such smuggling.

An underlying problem with both the salt and tea monopolies was one that still occurs today, that is, the problem of poorly defined policy. The officials and scholars writing at the time could not determine the purpose of these monopolies, as one historian notes:

> Throughout the Ming period, neither emperors nor officials seemed to have made authoritative statements of the exact purposes served by the salt and tea monopolies, and the exact procedures according to which the salt and tea administrations should operate. It was up to the discretion of individual officials to interpret the original intentions of the monopolies and how best to serve them[38].

The Wealth of Yangzhou: The seat of the Salt Administration

The wealth flowing into Yangzhou from the salt monopoly created opportunities for businesses in other industries. The wealthy merchants were free spenders and patronised a number of industries. A sizable market developed for cultural products, most notably books and paintings, creating opportunities for scholars and artists[39]. Courtesans and prostitutes felt their impact, as did other forms of entertainment including gardens, tea houses and brightly lit night markets.

The wealthy and powerful merchants invested in Yangzhou, creating a beautiful and cultured city, of which many remnants remain today. They created beautiful gardens and attracted many literati to the city. Scholars, poets and calligraphers all benefitted from their patronage. Displaying what today would be considered good corporate citizenship, the merchants also financed educational facilities, welfare centres, bridges, roads and firefighting services. They also played a key role in financing and managing famine relief granaries. Despite these good deeds, the salt merchants gained a reputation for extravagance. For example, a guidebook to Yangzhou describes how:

> . . . the salt merchants of Yang-chou vied with one another in extravagance. Each wedding or funeral, with all its expenses for food, clothing and carriage, cost several hundred thousand taels. There was one who insisted on having more than ten meticulously prepared dishes every meal. At dinner time, he and his wife were waited upon by a host of servants who served everything from tea and noodles to vegetable and meat plates. They only needed to shake their heads to have the undesired dishes removed and appetizing ones brought in . . .

There was one who erected wooden nude female statues in front of his inner halls, all mechanically controlled, so as to tease and surprise his guests . . .

There was one who wished to spend ten thousand taels in a single day. One of his guests suggested that he buy gold foils. From the tower on top the Golden Hill he threw down the gold foils which, carried by the wind, soon scattered amidst trees and grass and could not be gathered again.

There was another who spent three thousand taels buying pu-tao-weng [a kind of bottom-heavy doll in the form of an old man that never falls] from Soochou to be floated on water. So numerous were these dolls that the stream became choked.

There was one who loved beautiful things. From his gate-keepers to kitchen-maids only good-looking young persons were selected. On the other hand, there was one who was fond of ugly things. [Once an applicant,] being convinced from looking at the mirror that he was not ugly enough, smeared his face with soy sauce and exposed it to the sun. There was yet another who liked big things. He designed for himself a huge bronze urinal container five or six feet tall. Every night he climbed up to relieve himself.

For quite some while, these people vied with one another in novelties and eccentricities which were too numerous to be described in full[40].

Information on the great merchant families has survived; however, there is little detail on their individual business activities. One such family is the Ch'eng family who were noted for their wealth in the third quarter of the seventeenth century. The founder of the family fortune was Cheng Liang-ju, 'a head merchant of considerable ability'. Instead of dividing the business between his sons, he trusted his business to his eldest son, while three of his other five sons succeeded in getting a Confucian education. It was common practice for rich families to encourage their sons away from business, remembering that in Confucian China it was the scholar-official who sat at the top of the social hierarchy, while merchants were accorded the lowest rung. Consequently, as soon as a merchant could afford it, he would encourage the younger members of the family to gain an education and seek a career as an official.

In the case of the salt merchants, their wealth ensured that their children received the best educations in the empire. The family names of the great merchants can also be found among those receiving degrees at the time. It was a deliberate attempt to gain prestige and remove the stigma associated with having a merchant background. In fact, some families, on transitioning to scholar status, became strongly anti-commerce while others would have both merchants and scholars among their sons.

For example, the Ch'eng family's next generation produced two officials, while the business was once again given to the eldest son. The Ch'eng family participated in many of the cultural and social activities that characterised the merchant community of the time. Probably their most famous legacy is the bamboo garden of Yangzhou which they built to entertain the literati of the time. The garden still exists today and is one of Yangzhou's top tourist attractions.

Over time, the fortunes of Yangzhou's salt merchant families became diluted and squandered. Unlike the situation with the Ch'eng family, the most common practice on the death of the merchant was to divide the inheritance between the male heirs. This reduced the wealth that any one member possessed. Others experienced decline as a consequence of their extravagant spending. This could be seen in the observations of a late Ming scholar who compared the spending patterns of Huizhou merchants with those from Shanxi, saying:

The rich men of the empire in the regions south of the Yangtze are from Hsin-an [Hui-chou], in the regions north of that river from Shansi. The great merchants of Hui-chou have made fisheries and salt their occupation and have amassed fortunes amounting to one million taels of silver. Others with a fortune of two or three hundred thousand can only rank as middle merchants. The Shansi merchants are engaged in salt, silk, reselling, or grain. Their wealth even exceeds that of the former. This is because the Hui-chou merchants are extravagant, but those of Shansi are frugal. In fact, people of Hui-chou are also extremely miserly as to food and clothing . . . but with regard to concubines, prostitutes and lawsuits, they squander gold like dust[41].

Despite these weaknesses, the Huizhou merchants staked a claim as one of China's most successful merchant groups. Few, if any, groups could match them 'in terms of economic power, operation spectrum, capital amount, and talent'. They were deeply influenced by Confucianism, and acted with integrity in their operations. In chapter seven, we will consider this merchant culture in more depth, but first we must examine one of China's greatest industries.

CHAPTER 6

The China Industry

·············

All the potteries in the land are gathered there and the people
are numerous and the wealthiest in the whole province.[1]

Ming dynasty official Wang Shimao

While Chinese merchants were creating fortunes from distribution
and marketing, Chinese artisans were revolutionising production
techniques, and, in so doing, creating what was for centuries the
world's pre-eminent consumer industry. China produced a large
range of goods which it exported to the wider world. Its most important exports were tea and silk, but it was the third ranked export that
is of most interest, for this pioneered many of the features we associate with modern industry. This is the story of porcelain, a product
that provides us with another perspective of Chinese business: the
production of consumer goods.

Chinese porcelain was in yesteryear what the computer industry
is today. If you understood the production technology, you could
apply it to a vast range of products and applications. That included
products for cooking, eating and storage. Porcelain products were
everywhere – used for excreting and in religious rituals. Alternatively,
they might be purchased for their aesthetic and artistic qualities,
and, like similar products today, ownership was a status symbol
which spoke of the elite nature of its owner.

For centuries, China had a monopoly on this technology, which
allowed them to stride the world in a way that Apple and Microsoft do
today. Chinese porcelain was demanded throughout the world, and its
production reflected one of the earliest examples of multinational
commerce. Raw materials were imported to China from as far away as

Persia and added to the manufacturing process. The resulting products were sold across the world with markets in India, Egypt, Iraq and Persia. From the sixteenth century, porcelains were also exported to America via the Philippines and Acapulco, and in the seventeenth century, Europeans succumbed to a frenzy of chinoiserie.

At the heart of this global network was the town of Jingdezhen in Jiangxi province. It was the largest industrial complex producing consumer products in the world. It utilised methods of mass production centuries before they appeared in Western consumer industries. By contrast, European ceramics production of the time remained the craft of a single potter whose product never reached the sales or artistic quality of the Chinese.

For centuries, Chinese porcelain was the consumer industry par excellence. Such is the influence of this industry that even in the twenty-first century, many old women possess a China cabinet. The contents may not be from China, but their existence speaks of the influence that Chinese producers achieved.

How Did the Chinese Attain Such Success?

Ceramics are one of the oldest consumer items made by humans. Evidence has shown that mammoth hunters living during the Stone Age learned how to fire clay in bonfires and, in so doing, created the first ceramics[2]. This evidence was found in Moravia in the modern Czech Republic which reminds us that the Chinese were not the only producers. In fact, ceramic bowls and plates have been produced all around the world. So how, then, did the Chinese achieve such standout success?

To answer this question, we must have some basic understanding of ceramics. There are three types of ceramics. First is earthenware. This is the type of pottery found all over the world as it requires the least level of sophistication. Earthenware pots and bowls are made from clays that are easy to shape and do not need high-temperature kilns to make them hard. Earthenware bodies fire well at temperatures between 800 and 1,100 degrees Celsius[3].

Further up the scale is stoneware, a harder and stronger product which is attained in kilns that reach temperatures 1,200 to about 1,300 degrees Celsius. Finally, there is porcelain which differs in a number of ways. First, it fires at higher temperatures, 1,280 degrees upwards. Second, it does not just use one type of clay, but two. But most important is the result. Porcelain in a fired state is vitrified and translucent, delivering a product that is pure white or very pale grey[4].

To produce porcelain, one needs two things. First, it requires kilns that can produce high levels of heat that can be controlled to produce the desired outcomes. Second, it requires types of clay that can sustain such temperatures and produce the desired body. China was blessed with plentiful supplies of such clay in kaolin and petuntse, but it took time for the Chinese to develop suitable kilns.

The early Chinese ceramics industry underwent a number of innovations in kiln design. For example, one important innovation involved increasing the number of heat vents into the kiln chamber which enabled potters to more evenly distribute heat. Improvements in kiln design may have been a spillover from another industry that also used kiln technology, that is, metallurgy.

There was a close association between ceramics and metallurgy. They both used moulds and kilns and, during the Shang dynasty (1570–1045 BC), both produced objects for religious rituals. Ceramics were actually used in the production of bronze, particularly in the creation of moulds. Consequently, in the early years, the two industries developed together and helped create an efficient kiln technology[5]. Consequently, the ceramics workers who made the moulds for the bronze gained a full awareness of bronze production technology. Hence, it was a small step to apply that technology to ceramics.

As early as the Shang dynasty, the Chinese had created kilns capable of reaching temperatures as high as 1,200 degrees Celsius, a range that enables the creation of stoneware. By the Warring States period (475–221 BC), kilns could fire as high as 1,350 degrees Celsius, at which point porcelain can be created[6].

One innovation that enabled mass production was the advent of dragon kilns. The first of these appeared in the Zhou era (1045–256 BC). These kilns were built into hills, and used the slope of the hill to produce a natural draft and raise the heat generated. The largest dragon kilns stretched up slopes as much as 140 metres and could produce tens of thousands of porcelains in one firing.

During the following centuries, Chinese potters experimented and, through trial and error, gained knowledge of the potential of these technologies. Such lessons included how much oxygen to admit to the chamber, how to control the oxygen inflow, how different clays responded to different temperatures, and how best to manage the kiln process to reduce defects.

By the Tang dynasty (AD 618–907), Chinese potters had perfected the production of stoneware. As we read in earlier chapters, this was a time in which market activity was beginning to take off, so ceramics producers were well placed to profit from their knowledge. The industry blossomed with kiln complexes established in fifty counties in fifteen provinces, five times the number that existed in the previous dynasty[7].

Stoneware was a product far superior to the earthenware found in other parts of the world. It was significantly stronger, and consequently was in demand internationally. It found export markets in Indonesia, India, the Philippines, the Persian Gulf, the Red Sea and Egypt[8]. However, Tang potters did not rest on their success and continued to experiment and learn. They found that by adding kaolin to the clay, they could create a product that could withstand even higher temperatures without melting, and the product that came out of the kiln was a strikingly beautiful white. It was glass-like, vitrified with some translucence, but stronger and more durable than glass. This was porcelain, an industrial game-changer!

With this super-technology, Chinese potters were well equipped for the market expansion of the Song dynasty. When combined with growth in both population and foreign trade, many entrepreneurial potters set up new businesses. Of all the pottery kilns in China's history, 75 per cent of them were established in the Song dynasty. Porcelain manufacturers were soon operating throughout China, in one hundred and thirty counties in nineteen provinces[9].

The greatest output was in the north, as it was around the capital city of Kaifeng that the greatest wealth and richest clients came. Consequently, it was there that the better-quality products were made and the most innovation occurred. However, this changed in 1127 when the Jurchin Tartars invaded and occupied northern China. This caused the emperor's court to flee south and establish their capital at Hangzhou, in what became the Southern Song dynasty.

During the invasion, many northern kilns were destroyed and many potters fled south. The industry was dispersed throughout the country, but it was from around the market town of Longquan that the best work came. The kilns in this area produced a strong pale green product called 'celadon' which was exported throughout East Asia.

The Rise of Jingdezhen

Another region to experience growth in this time was around the town of Changnan in Jiangxi province. The town possessed no kilns. It was simply a market-centre where kilns in the region sold their product. A number of kilns operated in the nearby countryside but it was a secondary industry, with most labour devoted to farming. Kilns were scattered among the rural fields, and potters often spread their time between farming on the land that belonged to the kiln-owners as well as making pots[10].

In the early Song dynasty, the town received official recognition when the emperor Zhenzong purchased ceramics from it. As a consequence, it received a name change. The ceramics made for the emperor had 'made in the reign of Jingde' written on the base of the products. The word for market town was '*zhen*', so the town became 'Jingde-zhen', a name that would become synonymous with industrial excellence[11].

One official who spent time in Jingdezhen was Hong Yanzu (1267–1329). He was headmaster of the Changxiang Academy, and his experience inspired him to write the following poem about the town that turned mud into products and gave 'pleasure to people from all directions':

A single vessel completes my earlier purchases,
At once better and newer than earlier shapes.
From beginning to end a hundred artisans were involved,
Giving pleasure to people from all directions.
The abilities of carvers may be boundless,
But what purer transformations than those of soaking and
    rubbing?
Its impression is both red and purple;
We spend money like water on mud and dust![12]

Hong Yanzu was not the only scholar to write about porcelain. Other poets expressed their appreciation for porcelain and for what it enabled:

Into my porcelain cup, my servant pours my wine until it fills
    my feet, drowns my knees,
gathers around my waist and calms my heart until I can
    drink no more.
If I have more, it pours out, dripping out making a splashing
    sound, soaking my clothes and shoes.

The servant stands by and secretly smiles, making the host
and his guest change color[13].

The poems reflect a recognition that porcelain was a product admired by scholar-officials. At this stage, Jingdezhen was only one of many production areas, but the town was slowly transforming into a major industrial complex.

In the early fourteenth century, a revolution in Chinese porcelain occurred as a consequence of the globalisation of trade. The Mongol empire stretched from China to Islamic lands in the west, and with official encouragement of trade, many Islamic merchants came to China in search of profit. While they were impressed by the quality of Chinese porcelains, they wanted more colour. It was always possible to paint over a pot once it was made, but applying paint underneath the glaze could not be done reliably because the dyes could not handle the heat in the kilns.

In the foreign merchant's homelands, their inferior pottery was made to look more attractive by blue paint. Persia had deposits of cobalt ore that could sustain heat and created a beautiful blue. In order to create ceramics with the colours that their home market wanted, the merchants began transporting cobalt blue from their homelands to China. Hence, foreign demand and the potential of global transport links contributed to an innovation in Chinese porcelain production.

In a dynamic relationship, the Muslim merchants who came to Quanzhou and kiln owners in Jingdezhen built a global multinational commercial venture unprecedented in world history. Cobalt ore mined in Persia was shipped 8,000 kilometres to China, where products were custom-made for the Islamic market in the Middle East. To this day, some of the greatest collections of Yuan ceramics from Jingdezhen can be found in Iran's Ardabil shrine and in the Topkapi Seray in Istanbul.

This blue and white ware was made explicitly for the export market with designs and motifs ordered by the foreign merchants. In China, there was little demand for such colour. The Chinese consumer valued purity and perceived the bright blue as vulgar. It was not until well into the Ming dynasty that the Chinese began to embrace it, but with their own designs. The resulting products are among the most celebrated consumer products ever created, and today, a blue and white Ming vase can cost a fortune.

A Commercial Revolution at Jingdezhen

It was during this time that Jingdezhen underwent a radical transformation. The quality and quantity of product improved greatly, while the town itself emerged as a pre-eminent industrial centre. This was not a consequence of innovation in technique as there were no startling innovations[14]. There were refinements of technique like glaze blowing and the use of new colours, but these changes were not of a scale to result in the transformation that occurred. The revolution was one of commercial organisation.

A number of factors contributed to this transformation[15]. These included an increase in orders from the imperial court, changes in the supply of raw materials and labour, and new forms of management and finance. Overriding all of this was the increased commercialisation occurring in the Chinese economy during the sixteenth century. Jingdezhen was well placed to exploit these changes through its position on nationwide marketing and transportation networks.

Prior to this time, very little production actually occurred in Jingdezhen. It was a market town selling the output from kilns in the surrounding region. The rural kilns had benefitted from the rich supply of clay and timber that existed in the region, but their activities led to deforestation in the hills and thus they denied themselves a source of fuel. The industry relied on significant supplies of fuel in order to survive. An average kiln required 11,000 kilograms of wood when firing. A large one might use sixty-four tons a day[16]. To provide sufficient fuel, the region began importing timber down the Chang River, but this created a need for potters to be close to the transportation network. So they moved their operations to town. This also enabled quicker access to other imported supplies including limestone and fern, materials used for making glaze.

With expanded output, local clay deposits were also exhausted, and resources needed to be brought in from further afield[17]. The transportation network enabled the town to continue in the industry despite resource depletion. Furthermore, it expanded the range of materials that they could use, and eventually the town became reliant on imports for nearly all the raw materials for the porcelain industry[18].

The river also brought in other goods needed for the town to function, including consumer goods for the workers. Most important, the transportation network increased the size of the market that potters had access to. This was an important source of competitive advantage for the town. Jingdezhen had always been a market town, so it already had networks and capabilities which enabled it to link into and exploit the market growth occurring in China.

Another driver of industrialisation was the increased attention from the imperial court. The court had bought pottery from Jingdezhen as early as the Song dynasty, but purchases were irregular, and did not support a sustained investment. This changed in the Ming dynasty when imperial orders became larger and more regular.

In the Yuan dynasty, the government established a porcelain bureau in the town. As court patronage increased during the Ming dynasty, requirements expanded to include a fully staffed depot responsible for regulating the supply of imperial ware. The staff maintained quality control, organised shipments, and ensured production and delivery deadlines were met. The earliest commissioners heading the bureau were eunuchs and, as with any administrative position, their quality could vary. The first commissioner, Mang Shan, occupied the position for many years and had overseen large quantities of production. However, he ended up abusing his position, treating subordinates cruelly and redistributing imperial porcelain to his friends. In 1425, he was executed.

In some years, imperial orders for more than 400,000 pieces were received, which placed huge demands on an already busy production schedule. The imperial court were always given priority and a number of kilns were designated as suppliers for the emperor. If an order was placed that was beyond the capacity of these official kilns, other producers were drafted into service.

Although they were referred to as 'official kilns', they remained privately owned. They made imperial wares under contract. Later in the Ming dynasty, an imperial plant was created but it only existed temporarily. In the early Ming dynasty, there were three hundred kilns in the town. Twenty of these had imperial status in the Hongwu reign (1368–98), increasing to fifty-eight in the Yongle period (1402–24)[19]. When not working on imperial orders, they were free to manufacture for the market. This structure meant they had freedom to carry out commercial manufacturing but the government could apply firm control when they needed it. The history of the Chinese porcelain industry is principally one of private enterprise, but the quality demanded by the court must have helped in the development of high standards.

Jingdezhen's potters were entrepreneurs seeking profit. They either invested in a workshop or a kiln, or sometimes both. If they owned a kiln and a workshop, they could fire their own wares, as well as taking work in from other workshops[20]. This suggests there was a large amount of subcontracting in the industry. Different workshops specialised in different processes, so subcontracting would have increased the level of specialisation and raised the efficiency of the industry as a whole.

Like other Chinese businesses, these were family concerns, and the workshops often served as the house for the owner's family and his employees. Many were based around a single family, however, there was significant variation in the size of the kilns and workshops. Some kilns might employ tens or possibly hundreds of men. However, few establishments reached that size and the average was much lower[21].

Like any small business owner, the potters had to make decisions regarding hiring and firing of employees, taking on apprentices, wages and prices. Many of these decisions were determined by the guilds of Jingdezhen. Guilds acted like employers organisations, setting standards, demarcating boundaries between trades, and performing the various religious requirements[22].

There is some uncertainty as to the extent to which businesses existed where the managers were not the owners. There is evidence to suggest that some steps towards this modern business form may have been made. Ceramics historian Margaret Medley stated that many businesses were 'financed by commercial syndicates who capitalised production and thus ultimately owned the kilns'. A description of the industry from the early Qing dynasty would provide some support for this, stating, 'at present 20% or 30% of the potters are outsiders'[23].

From Jingdezhen, blue and white porcelain was carried on ships throughout East Asia, and into the Indian Ocean where it reached India, Egypt, Iraq and Persia. Indian Muslim traders distributed Chinese ceramics throughout the Indian Ocean. It was sought after by the Indian elite, including the Mughal emperor Shah Jahan who had his own impressive collection.

THE EUROPEAN MARKET

It was from the Indians that Europeans first acquired their regular imports. In 1497, the Portuguese king sponsored Vasco de Gama to sail down the African coast and into the Indian Ocean. Among the instructions he was given was one to purchase spices and porcelain. Two years later, he returned and presented the king with a dozen pieces of Chinaware. Such was their desirability, over the next three centuries, three hundred million products would make the journey to Europe[24]. No product in the world compared to Chinese porcelain. Its desirability can be seen in the following quote from a Portuguese cleric who, in 1563, described its quality to Pope Pius IV:

> In Portugal we call it porcelain. It comes from India and is made in China. The clay is so fine and transparent that the whites outshines crystal and alabaster, and the pieces which are decorated in blue dumbfound the eyes, seeming a combination of alabaster and sapphires . . .[25]

Before long, Europeans were bypassing India and trading directly with China. In 1513, Portuguese ships began reaching China, where ships were commonly loaded with 200,000 pieces of porcelain[26]. The European traders increasingly sent specific instructions to Jingdezhen describing the designs they wanted for their home market. It was custom-made production on a global scale.

During the sixteenth century, Spain was carving out its own global trading empire, and soon Chinese ceramics were being transported across the Pacific Ocean on the famed Manila Galleon. The ships sailed from the Philippines and across the Pacific Ocean to Mexico and Peru. When Spain took over Portugal, the Spanish crown controlled two trade routes from which the product could come, so it is not surprising that King Philip of Spain had the most impressive collection in Europe. By his death in 1598, he owned three thousand pieces including sauceboats, carafes, serving platters and wide-mouth jars[27].

While the Portuguese were the initial entrepreneurs in the European porcelain trade, their imports were not sold beyond their local market. It was the Dutch who brought porcelain to the rest of Europe. At the beginning of the seventeenth century, the Dutch were at war with the Spanish crown who, at that time, ruled both Spain and Portugal. So when a Dutch ship came across a Portuguese carrack, the *San Jago*, they captured it and seized its cargo. On board was a quantity of Chinese porcelain which was presented to the Dutch town Middleburgh. When a second carrack was captured in 1604, they decided to auction its porcelain cargo. The pieces reached high prices in the Amsterdam auction and sent a message that there was a significant demand for the product[28].

Soon, the Dutch East India Company (VOC) was travelling to China with ceramics being one of its principal cargoes. This cargo was named 'Kraak' porcelain after the carrack ships that provided the first products. Over the next two hundred years, the VOC carried at least 43 million pieces to Europe. However, the total sum coming to Europe was much higher as VOC employees working on the ships carried their own private shipments.

The English East India Company soon entered the market and, by 1662, settlers in the American colonies were also ordering porcelain from China. It says much about the flexibility and virtuosity of the Chinese producers that they could create custom-made designs for such a broad international clientele. They were commonly asked to decorate pieces with scenes from the Bible, Roman literature or European current events. For the Chinese potter who had never heard of Adam and Eve, or Neptune, such orders placed huge demands. To meet these custom-made orders, the potters were normally provided with models to copy. However, if even a little fault was found, a piece would be rejected and the Chinese would have to carry the cost. Consequently, European figures cost twice that of Chinese designs. The Jesuit priest Pere d'Entrecolles, who lived in Jingdezhen, described the reason for this:

... the porcelain that is sent to Europe is made after new models that are often eccentric and difficult to reproduce; for the least defect they are refused by the merchants, and so they remain in the hands of the potters, who cannot sell them to the Chinese, for they do not like such pieces. I have said that the difficulty of making certain models sent from Europe is one of the reasons why the pieces are so costly[29].

In the early eighteenth century, a complete dinner set, including customs duty, cost about £100 (approximately £14,000 today). The potters did not speak English and were dependent on the models and instructions sent to them. Sadly, mistakes sometimes got through as they copied the models. So, a client, having spent a small fortune and waited two years for a delivery, might open it expecting to see their family coat of arms on their porcelain. Instead, they might find the words 'Our coat of arms' or 'this colour is red' painted on every piece[30].

Despite the occasional mistake, Europeans looked upon the Chinese with envy. They had no idea how they made this product that was so superior to their local potteries. One publication that attempted to provide an answer showed the level of ignorance of the production technology:

A large mass of material composed of plaster, egg and oyster shell, of sea locusts and similar creatures is well mixed until it is of one consistency. It is then buried by the head of the family, who reveals the hiding place to one of his sons. It must remain in the ground for 80 years[31].

Marco Polo's book was not much help. He certainly had seen Chinese porcelain but he had no idea how it was made. He wrote the following of one porcelain centre:

Their dishes are made of a crumbly earth or clay which is dug as though from a mine, and stacked in huge mounds and then left for thirty or forty years exposed to the wind, rain and sun. By this time, the earth is so refined that dishes made of it are an azure tint with a very brilliant sheen. You must understand that when a man makes a mound of this earth, he does so for his children; the time of maturing is so long[32].

It seemed that porcelain would remain a Chinese monopoly as Europeans had no idea how to make it. However, in the early eighteenth century, Europeans gained the opportunity to plant a spy in Jingdezhen, in what has been called the earliest example of industrial espionage[33]. The spy was a Jesuit priest.

Industrial Espionage

In the sixteenth and seventeenth centuries, Spain and Portugal had carved out a trading network that stretched from South America in the west to China in the east. The Jesuit order had followed the traders, placing priests in the regions they settled. These international experiences provided Jesuits with a global knowledge as they acquired information from each of the countries they visited.

In the 1630s, Jesuit priests serving in Peru learned that the bark of the cinchona tree worked wonders on fever victims[34]. It was the source of quinine and greatly helped in the treatment of malaria. In 1691, the Chinese emperor Kangxi became afflicted with the disease, and a Jesuit priest by the name of Bouvet was on hand to treat him. Grateful for the service, Kangxi agreed to Bouvet's request to establish churches in China.

In March 1698, the ship *Amphitite* sailed from La Rochelle with ten Jesuit priests on board. On arrival in China, they were granted an audience with the emperor before being sent to their posts. One of the priests, thirty-five-year-old Francois Xavier d'Entrecolles (1664–1741), was posted to Jingdezhen where he was tasked with establishing a church. He was also asked to send information on the porcelain industry. In 1712, he sent a lengthy letter to Louis-Francois Orry, the treasurer of the Jesuit Mission. His letter begins:

> From time to time I have stayed in Qing-tê-chên to administer to the spiritual necessities of my converts, and so I have interested myself in the manufacture of this beautiful porcelain, which is so highly prized, and is sent to all parts of the world. Nothing but my curiosity could ever have prompted me to such research, but it appears to me that a minute description of all that concerns this kind of work might, somehow, be useful in Europe[35].

He also explains how he gained the information:

> Besides what I myself have seen, I have learnt a great many particulars from my neophytes, several of whom work in porcelain, while others do a great trade in it. I also confirmed the truth of the information they had given me by a study of the Chinese books on the subject, so that I believe I have obtained a pretty exact knowledge of all that concerns this beautiful art, so that I can talk about it with some confidence. Among these books I examined the history of Fou-liang, and I have read carefully, in the fourth volume, the article on porcelain[36].

Although he has been described as an industrial spy, this description suggests that d'Entrecolles is best described as a researcher. There seems to be no hint of secrecy or deception. In fact, the Chinese freely gave him information, and he made many friends among his contacts.

D'Entrecolles's first letter goes into substantial detail about the town and its industry. However, the letter did not contain enough information for French potters to make porcelain. He was told to provide more. In 1722, he sent another letter, and this contained the missing detail identifying the importance of the two clays, kaolin and petuntse, that were used together to form porcelain.

While d'Entrecolles was in China, efforts to discover the secret of porcelain continued to occupy European rulers. One nineteen-year-old German to be roped into the process was a self-proclaimed alchemist named Johann Friedrich Bottger. In 1701, he gained a reputation in central Europe for his ability to transmute silver into gold. He was, of course, a charlatan, but his claims brought him to the attention of King Augustus of Saxony who put him under detention and ordered him to deliver the gold he claimed he could create. When this failed, he was put to work on another project – finding the secret of porcelain. He was forced to work with Ehrenfried Walther von Tschirnhaus, who had studied mathematics and medicine at the University of Leiden. Together, they experimented on different types of clays in what has been described as 'the first research and development enterprise in history'[37].

In 1709, their efforts bore fruit as they finally found the right mix of clays. Soon, beds of kaolin were discovered in Saxony and this enabled the king to open the first European porcelain enterprise: the Royal Saxon porcelain manufacture at Meissen. The Germans still had much to learn about building and managing kilns, and the capabilities of the clays. Nevertheless, the Europeans learned quick and by 1760, thirty porcelain manufacturers had been established in Europe.

Back in China, d'Entrecolles had no idea that the Germans had already solved the puzzle. Nevertheless, his attempts to aid technology transfer were not wasted. His letters contained valuable information, and Josiah Wedgwood, who established the ceramics tradition in England, studied them for knowledge on production techniques.

D'Entrecolles' letters described how the town possessed three thousand kilns, the largest industrial complex in the world at the time. One of the most startling facts he revealed was the efficiency with which they operated and the level of specialisation that existed in these works. D'Entrecolles stated:

> It is surprising to see the rapidity with which these vessels pass through so many different hands; and I am told that a piece of fired porcelain has passed through the hands of seventy workmen[38].

Compared to Europe, where a single potter was involved in every part of the production process, the idea of having so many workers, each specialising in one part of the process, gave an indication of how the Chinese obtained such high quality. Consider d'Entrecolles' description of painting:

> The painting is distributed in the same workshop among a great number of workmen. One workman does nothing but draw the first colour line beneath the rims of the pieces; another traces flowers, which a third one paints; this man is painting water and mountains, and that one either birds or other animals[39].

This high division of labour and resulting efficiency bears great similarities to American production in the twentieth century, when businesses followed the thinking of F. W. Taylor and the school of scientific management. The Chinese did not have an automated assembly line, but the principles of production were the same.

In the same way that Americans used specialisation to mass produce and create many standardised products, the Chinese, too, would often make many reproductions of one product. To give an idea of the number of products being processed, the largest kilns held 100,000 pieces. It must have been very boring to paint the same design on thousands of identical cups and plates, but such numbers allowed the painters to become very adept at a design which reduced the number of mistakes they made and increased their speed.

Specialisation did not just occur inside the works. Businesses might also specialise in certain types of product such as lanterns, fish bowls, wine cups and storage jars. As with many modern manufacturers, people often worked in shifts. The largest kilns could fire as long as a week, and needed to be continually supervised during that time.

Not all production was on a mass scale as specialised orders often came through, especially from the imperial court. Foreign customers also tested the town's innovation skills, as foreign buyers demanded shapes or designs that the Chinese had never seen before. Time and time again, the workers were equal to the task, and in so doing helped build the largest industrial complex in the world. The industry was capable of great virtuosity and innovation[40].

In any market economy, it is common for a worker who has gained experience working for an employer to consider starting their own business. However, not everyone who takes this step succeeded, as d'Entrecolles explains:

For one workman who gets rich there are a hundred others who ruin themselves, though they still try their fortunes further in the hope that they may save enough to become shopkeepers[41].

Some would try their fortunes further afield. D'Entrecolles described how many workmen set up operations in Fujian and Canton hoping to supply the European traders in these ports, but the quality of the product was not as good as Jingdezhen:

Some workmen of Qing-to-chen formerly transported themselves and their materials there, hoping to make considerable profit by reason of the great European commerce at Amoy, but this scheme came to naught, as they were not successful in their manufacture[42].

MARKETING AND DISTRIBUTION

Porcelain was produced for two specific markets in Jingdezhen. First were the official wares produced for the imperial court. Official ware was the highest-quality product and was produced to meet specific designs demanded by the court. It would be used as palace decoration, gifts to senior officials or for exchange in the international tribute trade[43].

The rest of the produce was produced for sale on the commercial market to privately owned businesses and individuals. This included a large variety of consumers from officials and wealthy landowners who might demand fine porcelain and antique reproductions, down to the poorer people who bought simple pottery for everyday use[44].

The vast majority of product was sold inside Jingdezhen with very little transported out of the town before it was sold. This applied to both retail shops who sold smaller amounts to individual consumers or branches of wholesale buyers who sold in bulk. Retail shops were normally small family businesses that sold lower-quality ware to the clients who visited them throughout the year. These shops were located on Porcelain Street, 'a thoroughfare devoted entirely to the sale of porcelain . . .'[45].

The largest and most important trade was that conducted with the wholesalers. Because of the size of their orders, wholesalers normally had to order three to four months in advance to give the manufacturers time to make the order. To help them, they relied on brokers who acted as middle men between the wholesalers and manufacturers. A 25 per cent deposit would be given to the broker who would bargain with sellers, send for samples and arrange the details of the sale. Brokers were licensed by the government and provided confidence to both buyer and seller. A Qing dynasty writer describes the important role they performed:

Dealers wishing to buy porcelain are introduced by brokers. The price is discussed, a future purchase is arranged, and the transaction is complete. On the prearranged date when taking delivery, the dealer must, by way of proof, hold a ticket showing the number of articles ordered. If any of the goods to be carried away have blemishes or confused colours they are nonetheless reckoned among the number recorded on the ticket and on being handed to the potter will be exchanged for sound ones. This is called an 'exchange ticket'. The porcelain ticket and the 'exchange ticket' are both made of plain paper. They will either be stamped with the name of the potter's establishment and the number of pieces will be added in writing or the whole thing will be written in ink[46].

When a merchant arrived in Jingdezhen, he would immediately go to a broker who dealt with merchants from his area. Jingdezhen was home to fifty or sixty brokerage firms that were organised into groups representing a specific geographic area. For example, if a merchant from Zhejiang arrived in town, 'he would make contact with a broker who dealt with his province, stay at the broker's home . . . and arrange all his dealings through him'[47].

Merchants came from all over China to purchase supplies at Jingdezhen. Some might only buy enough cups and bowls to fill a large basket, which they carried home and sold for a quick profit. Others purchased significantly larger orders which they then distributed through nationwide commercial networks.

The most prominent of these were the merchants from Huizhou who we discussed in the previous chapter. They had already established networks of travelling merchants, storekeepers, brokers and other middlemen needed for distribution. If one of their merchants brought rice, timber, cotton, silk and tea to Jingdezhen, they would soon recognise the opportunities for adding porcelain to their books. In so doing, they carved out new markets for the Jingdezhen potter. From the late Ming and early Qing dynasties, Jindezhen ceramics could be found all over China, thanks to the activities and connections of the Huizhou merchants.

Together, the potters of Jingdezhen and the Huizhou merchants brought value to the Chinese people and beyond. In return, they built great wealth. The dynamic nature of this market was described by Qing dynasty magistrate Chen Yu:

There is one town, Jingde, a large urban area in the south of the county. As for its line of business, this is where the potters and the ceramics traders are. Within the seas, we have the use of these ceramics and amass the profits generated through ceramics. Boats and carts crowd together here, merchants and traders rush about, people from the five directions intermingle, all spreading out their wares, so numerous, it is truly magnificent![48]

CHAPTER 7

Merchant Culture in the Late Ming and Qing Dynasties

....

The commercial revolution that began in the late Ming generated great wealth in China. This was observed by a party of Koreans who got shipwrecked in China in 1488. The head of this group, Ch'oe Pu, described the bustling commercial activity he observed at Hangzhou:

> The markets pile up gold and silver; the people amass beautiful clothes and ornaments. Foreign ships stand as thick as the teeth of a comb, and in the streets wine shops and music halls front directly each on another[1].

More people were making money and there was more to spend it on. However, this new-found wealth did not flow evenly, a phenomenon that threatened Confucian concepts of equity. This emphasis on wealth was the antithesis of Confucian thought, as was the changing social structure of society. People's value should not be measured in money, but by their knowledge and contribution to society. Consequently, this transition to a commercial, market economy was not welcomed by all, as one Ming scholar expressed:

> As merchants and traders became more numerous, farming was not emphasized. Property was exchanged. Prices fluctuated. Those who were able were successful. Those who were a bit slow were ruined. The family on the east might become rich while the family on the west was impoverished. As the equilibrium between those of higher and lower status was

lost, everyone struggled over paltry sums. People were mutually exploitive; each sought to further himself. Thereupon, deceptive practices sprouted, contentions arose, recreations were off-color, extravagance was everywhere[2].

Anxieties over these changes reinforced the poor view that officialdom held of commerce, and many clung to traditional Confucian views that denigrated merchants. However, the extent that this stigma affected business operations varied over time. In the early Ming period merchants suffered dearly, but the late Ming ushered in a commercial freedom equal to that in the Song dynasty. By the Qing dynasty, merchants were gaining a new visibility and respectability[3]. Officials increasingly showed a willingness to accommodate business activity.

This new respect for business could be seen in a number of ways. Elite households were comfortable having one son working as a scholar-official, while another son pursued a career in commerce. Many eligible examination candidates actually dropped their studies to pursue opportunities that were opening in commerce. Buddhist monasteries that previously shied away from naming merchant benefactors, now openly named businessmen who donated to them. New terminology was introduced to capture this changing outlook. The word for merchant (*shang*) was joined to the word for gentry (*shen*) to form 'gentry-merchant' or 'gentleman-merchant' (*shangshen*).

Even the officials who wrote official documents showed respect for the gentleman-merchants. For example, 'salt gazetteers' were originally written as records of the Salt Administration, providing maps and regulations for each salt-producing region. But in the Qing dynasty, their nature changed. More information was included on regional customs and lores, but more importantly, they also included biographies of outstanding salt merchants. These merchants would be described under titles such as 'filiality and friendship', 'generous deeds', and 'respect for uprightness'. These descriptions are normally associated with scholar-officials and a Confucian education. This indicated that not only were the merchants gaining in prestige, they were doing it by acting within the Confucian value system[4].

The fact that officials could write kindly on merchants also revealed an increased closeness between the two groups. One reason why officials were increasingly receptive to business is that many of them came from merchant families. Their families' wealth enabled them to get the best education, and pass the exams that paved the way for a career in officialdom. But even if the merchants' children did not complete their exams, their higher education put them at an intellectual level which facilitated interaction between the two groups. Officials could hear and see the benefits of trade and wrote reports on them, such as the one referred to in chapter five by Zhang Han.

Merchants benefitted from close friendships with officials and nurturing such relationships was a deliberate business strategy. Merchants benefitted from these relationships in a number of ways. First, they gained political protection from unfair pressure. Second, such relationships might help them attain better commercial arrangements in industries with significant government intervention. Finally, merchants gained public prestige from associating with scholar-officials[5].

Chinese education was based on Confucian principles so, with so many merchants gaining a Confucian education, it was bound to impact on the mentality of merchants at the time. Historians studying the late Ming and Qing dynasties have noticed how the merchant culture was increasingly shaped by Confucian values. However, it is wrong to ascribe this trend only to education. It also reflected a drive for legitimacy and respect, with merchants trying to overcome their traditional low status. At the same time, scholar-officials had to come to terms with the increasing commercialisation of society. If business was conducted ethically, the conflict in values would be less obvious. The result was a business culture with an emphasis on Confucianism[6]. This placed an ethical framework around commercial behaviour and acted as a guide for merchant action.

This trend was noted by Richard Lufrano, an expert in Asian history at the City University of New York. He studied business culture of the time and noted that the merchant ideology was characterised by the concept of 'self-cultivation'. In his book *Honorable Merchants*, Lufrano noted that this process of self-cultivation, which had roots in Confucianism, 'involved learning how to deal with people and live to cultivate appropriate personality traits'[7]. In so doing, merchants would become more disciplined and exhibit wiser judgement which would help them avoid many of the pitfalls that could trap a businessman. Such behaviour also helped reinforce merchants' standing as reputable gentlemen.

Other historians have come to similar conclusions. For example, Timothy Brook from the University of British Columbia noted that Confucian ideals actually helped business performance. If a business is to succeed in the long term, merchants must act with honesty, not deceit. Similarly, a merchant needed to be prudent, acting with caution in business dealings. Some of the other Confucian values found in merchants included an emphasis on family and relationships[8], as well as fairness, that is, not making profit through immoral behaviour[9].

Another value and behaviour that became more prominent through this period is that of 'happiness through doing good works' (*leshan haoshi*)[10]. This value emphasised charity and philanthropic works. The gazettes written by government officials frequently described charitable works of merchants. The gazettes spoke of exemplary moral behaviour by businessmen, and illustrated how the gap in values between Confucianism and business was closing.

This practice of 'happiness through doing good works' could be seen among the wealthiest Huizhou merchants, including those operating in the salt trade. For example, a salt merchant by the name of Geng Hui Ying Zhang is recorded as having donated coffins and jackets to those in need, and provided funds for building a temple. He provided food for the starving and shelter for the homeless, and medicines during an epidemic. The lives he is said to have saved were 'countless'[11]. Another gazette provides a biography of a Mr Wang who made his fortune in the late Ming dynasty:

Mr. Wang liked to help people and to give assistance to the poor. If anyone among his kinsmen could not afford a funeral for his parents, Mr. Wang would always buy some land and build a tomb for him. As soon as he heard someone could not make ends meet, land to rent to him [sic]. Whenever he was out traveling and met some unburied spirit, he would bid his servants bury it and present some offerings[12].

The gazette provides other examples of Mr Wang's kindness including helping provide relief during food crises and providing funds to repair damaged village bridges[13]. It was common for merchants to fund local works, particularly the building and repair of temples. Merchants often worked with officials in leading charitable acts and it was not just the wealthiest merchants who engaged in such behaviour. For example, one official wrote that when a large number of vagrants arrived unexpectedly in his district, shop owners helped out and provided rice for the soup kitchens, firewood and silver.

Charitable works and disaster relief might not necessarily be done in conjunction with the officials. A merchant might act of his own accord. For example, one gazette describes how the merchant Wu Min Yin felt for the starving people in his community, so filled a boat with wheat which was distributed to them. On another occasion, after a nearby water disaster, he encouraged other merchants to join him and give food to those affected. His biography praises him as a righteous man who is quoted as saying:

> How could I not be ashamed if I did not willingly donate the grain from my granaries in times of distress to those living in my native place?[14]

Guilds

Another feature of Chinese business that reinforced the business culture and influenced business practice was the guilds. We can trace their origins to the Tang dynasty markets where businesses were placed in rows of the same trade. Hence, guilds are referred to by the Chinese name for rows, '*hang*'.

Guilds existed for different industries and crafts from paper manufacturers to candle makers. They represented their industry when dealing with the government and, in later years, took over many regulatory functions that the government had previously performed. Guilds administered price controls, registered craftsmen and merchants, and collected levies on trade[15]. They determined rules for a number of aspects of each trade including the length of apprenticeships (normally three years). They also provided standard measures for their trade which helped inspire confidence in business transactions with the public. For example, a Suzhou 'foot' was used when measuring Suzhou silk.

Guilds did not only cover producers and craftsmen. They were also created to govern the work of traders. Merchant guilds came to prominence in the Song dynasty and reached their peak in the Ming and Qing dynasties[16]. The earliest merchant guilds were comprised of traveling merchants who came from the same region and provided an element of protection when they travelled to distant markets. They provided security and welfare support for their members. Mutual aid was a common component of all guilds who helped their members if they experienced misfortune[17].

Guilds built meeting places which became centres of business activity. They provided accommodation for visiting merchants and secure storage facilities. Consistent with the time, the guilds would also have a patron deity. In a world where success could be determined by fate, guild-members took their religion seriously, and this could be a powerful force in enforcing moral behaviour. For example, the 1828 rules for the Peking Dyestuffs Guild warned: 'Be cautious. Take Care. If our investigations do not reveal those who, with evil heart, have violated the guild regulations then the gods will find them out and cease to aid them.'[18]

In the early days, guild culture was weak and vague but, over time, rules and guidelines were developed to provide mutual protection and reduce the risks associated with trade. Guilds were the governing bodies for their members and their duties included solving disputes between members. Consequently, they became concerned with promulgating ethical business practices. Accepted criteria of conduct emerged which were reinforced by the guild's culture. There might be variation, but their common ethical basis included honesty and credibility, appropriateness, and moral qualities derived from Confucianism[19].

If members accepted these values it would help create what economists call 'social capital' which has been described as 'the links, shared values and understandings in society that enable individuals and groups to trust each other and so work together'[20]. A wider sense of trust gives people confidence to conduct business and provides the basis for a strong economy. Unsurprisingly, the guilds stressed honesty and credibility. A merchant should be honest with their employees, customers and suppliers. This also had reputational benefits for the merchants. A merchant should also have integrity and keep to his/her word. This would facilitate the development of trust.

In later years, guilds were known for the restrictions that they placed on trade. They endeavoured to provide each member a stable income based on social harmony and a just profit. This clearly reflects a Confucian value system; however, in practice it meant a reduction in competition, with restrictions on newcomers entering the trade and strong prohibitions against one member undercutting another in price or increasing market share at another member's expense[21]. Such restrictions did not encourage innovation and had a serious impact on China's economic growth. It stands in sharp contrast to the highly competitive business environment developing in the West which was producing innovations on a daily basis. To Westerners, Chinese guild restrictions were absurd, as is illustrated in this satirical attack on the barber's guild:

> Barbers . . . are in many parts of the country forbidden to add that art of shampooing to their ordinary craft, it having been determined by the union that to shampoo was beneath the dignity of the knights of the razor. During the last six days of the year, when the heads of the whole male portion of the empire are shaved, barbers are forbidden to clean the ears of their customers, as it is their wont to do during the rest of the months. Anyone found breaking this rule is liable to be mobbed, and to have his tools and furniture thrown in to the street[22].

Merchant Manuals

Another valuable source of information on business culture and practice can be found in the manuals that were written for and sold to merchants of the time. The first business books were route books that provided instructions on how to travel safely between specific destinations. The target market for these books included both merchants and gentry who at times travelled in the course of their work.

An example of such a book is the *Encyclopedia for Gentry and Merchants* written in the Ming dynasty by Cheng Chunyu. Included in this book was a description of the route from Huizhou to Jingdezhen, a route that Huizhou merchants would take if they were dealing in porcelain. The book described overland paths and the landmarks along the way. It described river crossings and places where it was necessary to take a boat, and it told of inns and post stations where one could rest on the way to Jingdezhen[23].

Merchant manuals were themselves examples of the expanding market activity and the opportunities that existed for entrepreneurs. There was a boom in publishing and many entrepreneurs set up companies in this industry. They used woodblock printing technology which had very low capital costs. The books were carved on to blocks which could be used to reprint any number of books with the only additional cost being labour, paper and ink. With growing wealth in the economy, more and more consumers had the purchasing power to buy books including encyclopaedias, fiction and morality books.

There was also a growing demand for business books. As the economy expanded between the sixteenth and nineteenth centuries, approximately 30,000 new markets were created. People who understood commercial practice could exploit the opportunities that came with such growth, and this meant a demand existed for books on commercial techniques. These books were written and published for the same reasons that business books are written today. They targeted consumers who wanted to harness economic opportunity[24].

The books discussed business practices that would help merchants and tradesmen recognise and avoid hazards prevalent in the Chinese business environment. They provided technical knowledge in areas as diverse as financial management, employment of staff, understanding market fluctuations, the use of credit and recognising criminal schemes. These technical issues were underlined with a need for self-cultivation and character training consistent with Confucianism[25].

Books were published that targeted specific aspects of business, an example being *The Merchant's Guide (Shanggu bianlan)*. The author, Wu Zhongfu, stated that when he went to a bookstore, he noticed that there was nothing available for shopkeepers. Recognising a gap in the market, he responded by writing his book. Another example of targeting specific business practice is the manual *Essential Pawnbroking (Dianye xuzhi)*, written in the late Qing dynasty for apprentices in the pawn trade.

The motives for publishing were the same in yesteryear as they are today – profit – but it was not the only motive. All the authors had a desire to teach Confucian morality and promote a culture of self-cultivation. The manuals stressed that by practising the values of the Confucian gentleman, merchants would increase their likeliness of obtaining success and wealth[26]. If a merchant practised high moral qualities and engaged in socially accepted practices, he could enhance his social status[27]. We find in manuals such as *Essentials for Tradesmen (Gongshang qieyao)* the values of benevolence, righteousness, propriety, moral knowledge and sincerity were stressed. Similarly, the manual *Solutions for Merchants (Keshang yilan xingmi)* repeatedly referred to the principles that provided the basis of Confucian society[28].

However, a question that must be considered is 'do the manuals accurately reflect Chinese commercial practice or are they examples of Confucians pushing their values on merchants?' A modern equivalent might be a business book written by an expert on ethics. Nevertheless, most historians today 'agree that actual merchants wrote the Qing merchant manuals and that these guidebooks accurately reflect the commercial world and the merchant mentality at the time'[29]. The manuals might reflect an ideal, but it is an ideal that merchants genuinely strived for.

However, we cannot assume that these values reflected all merchants' behaviour. The books are all imbued with the Confucian ethic which would reflect the education of the authors and the more successful merchants, but it might not reflect lower level merchants. Most merchants did not possess Confucian educations and civil service degrees. The majority of businesses were small family businesses and employed only a few apprentices and clerks[30]. Nevertheless, much of the advice in these books makes common sense given the business environment.

THE NEED FOR RIGHTEOUSNESS AND PROPRIETY

It has actually been claimed that one of the reasons why Huizhou merchants were so successful was because of the influence of Confucianism on their business practices. This argument suggests that, as the economy became more complex, the intellectual requirements of a businessman became more important, and someone with Confucian education had the superior analytical and organisational skills needed[31].

The marketplace was full of danger for someone setting out in business during the fifteenth to nineteenth centuries. Those dangers included both market uncertainties and criminal actions, so the merchant manuals gave useful advice on how to avoid them. Crime could occur in many different ways. One common area of trickery occured when payment is made in silver, hence the manuals stress the need to check the silver before it is handed over. The manuals described what to look for in silver to confirm its purity. This required a full examination of the ingot from its base to its rim, finding out where it came from and where it was produced. If there was any doubt, the ingot should be cut in two to ensure that it did not contain copper.

A merchant's job required a lot of travel and the manuals are full of advice for merchants undertaking a journey. The books described different journeys and identified whether a trade route was dangerous or not. Some routes may be dangerous because of the terrain, while others were plagued by thieves. A 1792 manual entitled *Essentials for the Artisan and Merchant* warned against taking short cuts even if a local recommends it. If a merchant was unfamiliar with a route, he could end up getting lost, hungry and tired: 'Walking on a road, do not greedily take a short cut', as you will end up 'bitter for having ever taken the short cut'[32].

The manual also advises great care when hiring people to help carry goods and wares. A merchant travelling across country usually needed to hire others to help transport their goods. Great care was needed in the selection of these people, lest they turn on the merchant in the middle of the journey.

Travelling by boat was particularly dangerous and a merchant had to watch out for other passengers. The *Shanggu bianlan* warns that if other passengers did not have much luggage they may not be legitimate travellers but thieves. In which case, the merchant needed to be very careful. It wasn't just passengers who posed dangers. Sometimes the crew could not be trusted.

The *Essentials for the Artisan and Merchant* warned that 'many boats gang up to swindle you, you must see through this'[33]. The manual described an elaborate scheme in which boatmen and accomplices would scam the merchant. Halfway through the boat trip, the boat would be boarded by 'officials' who would take the goods and threaten the merchant with arrest. In reality the officials were bandits operating in league with the boatmen. The manual states, 'You will think, wrongly, that you have been subject to an actual disaster, and be grateful that you were not arrested. Please take note of this experience'[34].

An important form of protection came from the ability to judge people's character. A businessman needed to be able to identify whether a person was dishonest or would take advantage of them. The *Shanggu xingmi* gave some indications on how this could be done. A merchant needed to pay close attention to the speed with which someone answered questions, or whether they looked directly at you or looked from side to side. If they wanted to talk to you in private, it meant they did not want others to hear, which suggests they were trying to trick you. Similarly, the *Maoyi xuzhi* says that when lending money, a businessman should be wary of those using 'sweet words'[35].

While the manuals warned merchants to be on the lookout for immoral people, they stressed that merchants must not operate the same way. Profit must be made honestly without exploitation. Consistent with Confucian thinking, the *Shanggu xingmi* argues that it is better to be poor and free of guilt than profit from misery and dishonesty[36].

BUILDING A STABLE BUSINESS

Many risks in business occurred because of the inherent instability of markets. Prices were capable of wild fluctuation depending on weather, the state of crops or the state of trade routes. As the *Shishang yaolan* noted, prices 'go up and down and are never regular'[37]. The strategies used by a merchant needed to take into account the inherent instability of markets. This meant using strategies that reduced risk.

This uncertainty and variability reinforced the need for caution and prudence that Confucian scholars stressed. The handbooks advised merchants to avoid the temptation of get-rich-quick schemes. Success was not made overnight 'but through long, slow, steady profits'[38]. The manuals advised merchants to take the 'middle way', a concept found in both Confucian and Taoist thought. These philosophies stressed the path of moderation. This path provided the stability that merchants sought – 'how could one not be happy?'[39]

This advice had value, not just for philosophical reasons, but also for practical reasons. In a world of great market variability, a merchant put himself in danger if he took too many risks. As the *Shanggu xingmi* argued, 'one who takes excessive risk will collapse, one who maintains a just medium will be level and stable'[40]. A merchant should be happy with profits of 20 to 30 per cent, while profits of 70 to 80 per cent were not sustainable. A merchant who gave in to greed was putting his business at risk.

The manual entitled *Essentials for Gentlemen and Merchants* (*Shishang yaolian*) stressed the importance of timing. A merchant could lose everything if they did not act at the correct time, hence it states 'do not mistake the time, when to do trade'[41]. Another transla-tion, *Essentials for Gentry and Merchants* (*Shishang leiyao*), argued that the key to timing was knowledge:

> There is much uncertainty in business. Prices are not steady.
> One needs to know when to buy and sell. One needs to know
> people and if they are good or bad[42].

The *Shanggu xingmi* stated that stability was the ultimate aim of Chinese business. Stability was a sign of a gentleman – 'be stable for this is the way of the gentleman'[43]. Stability was also a sign of tight financial management. Consequently, a skill that contributed to the long-term success of a business was care with handling money. This means regularly monitoring your accounts and reigning in your expenses, as one manual stated:

There are the diligent and lazy, the extravagant and the frugal. From the time one rises in the morning, one should be watchful over business, one should be diligent, frugal, and not detest being humble. When midday arrives the businessman should look at serious books and review his accounts[44].

A business with tight control over expenses would more easily survive business downturns, so it is no surprise to see business manuals claiming that frugality contributes to stability. A sense of frugality was crucial for long-term success and should be instilled early in the education of young businessmen. The *Maoyi xuzhi* advised that an apprentice businessman should:

> ... work in a small shop. He will only wear cheap clothes, eat only coarse rice, drink insipid tea. He will realize that he cannot waste, that he can only be industrious and thrifty and cannot be indulgent in luxurious and expensive habits. He will have to heed his ordinary everyday daily expenses. After seeing this way of living, he will know making money is not easy[45].

In this way, the apprentice learned the true value of money. It took time to earn but could be spent in an instant. As the *Encyclopedia for Gentry and Merchants* states, 'Wealth does not come into one's hands easily; when you use it, think about the difficulty of earning it.'[46]

Many manuals stressed the concept of *liangru weichu* (expenses should not exceed income) and that businessmen should live within their means. Frugality was a key characteristic of businessmen and an important ingredient for success: 'the frugal are virtuous, whereas the wasteful and extravagant will find it hard to succeed'[47]. Those businessmen who failed to use their money with caution were inviting danger. The manual *Shanggu xingmi* contained an aptly titled *Song of Caution* which warned of the need to save and avoid reckless spending. Such behaviours led to failure: 'the cause of being in destitute and humble circumstances is waste and extravagance'[48].

It was human nature for a businessman, on becoming rich, to change his spending patterns, but the manuals warned 'do not change your standards once rich, do not be greedy . . . you need to keep your money'[49]. The *Dianye xuzhi* warned that it was easy to become accustomed to an extravagant lifestyle, which could be hard to shake during economic downturns. It could lead to borrowing, debt, or even worse, it may lead the businessman to engage in unethical behaviours that bring shame to the family.

Manuals repeatedly advised merchants not to be greedy and to avoid unnecessary expenditure, but financial management went beyond that to include financial planning: 'If when using money you have no plan, then gradually your wealth will be eroded'[50]. A businessman must know the limits of his expenditure in advance, otherwise he may not be able to meet his other obligations:

> Some think they do not need to calculate their expenses and do not need to save a lot, and are particular about what they eat and drink, but how can they provide for their parents?[51]

FAMILY AND RELATIONSHIPS

The need for frugality and long-term planning was linked to the familial nature of Chinese businesses and Confucian thought. Tight financial control was important for a business's survival. It was therefore a businessman's duty to be frugal so that the business could be passed on to the next generation of the family. A businessman who acted otherwise risked bringing shame upon his family. By contrast, a frugal businessman learned the value of money and brought honour to his family. When going on business trips, the *Dianye xuzhi* advises merchants to watch their expenses:

> When leaving home and going far away, you need to be careful with money to not easily waste and also to have your family in the forefront of your mind. One should clothe and eat simply, and remember your parents[52].

The family was central to Confucian philosophy and in the *Shanggu xingmi*, the main aim of life and business was to support the family. The family must come before the business.

> . . . if a man cannot manage a family, he will not be successful. If he is not good at managing a family, no matter what other capacity he has, he is useless[53].

Advice in the manuals reflect the Confucian concept of filial piety. The duties of children to their parents were outlined and stressed the need to obey and respect their authority:

> On family . . . you must be filial. When parents get old, you must act respectfully. When they are afraid, you must show no fear. When their strength is weak, you must support them. When they are hungry you must feed them. When they are cold you must provide them clothes of silk[54].

The manuals also give advice on how to bring up children, and how to integrate them into the family business. A parent showed their love to their children, not by showering them with gifts, but by giving them less money to 'make them know that it is difficult to get money'[55]. They should not be brought up accustomed to luxury, and the parents should school their children in the family business:

. . . if you do not teach the child the family business then he will become accustomed to luxury and extravagance. He will be arrogant and conceited. He will not know the difficulty of making money or wealth and will spend at will. He will not have the tradesman's heart[56].

A businessman's relationships were not limited to his family. Success was strongly influenced by his ability to manage relationships with external parties. This is commonly known as *guanxi* which refers to the cultivation of personal relationships. The manuals give important advice on who these relationships should be with. For example, the *Shanggu xingmi* stressed the need to associate with people of high character. Friends of low character could lead you astray whereas those of high character would have a positive moral effect:

Even if you have a lot of money, you will lose it, if you have bad friends. So how can you say that you have money when you have bad friends?[57]

There is one type of relationship that merchants should be particularly wary of; that is, sexual and romantic love. The *Shanggu xingmi* warns of women whose speech will 'have no shame' in attempting to seduce a man[58]. If the merchant is overwhelmed by desire, he may indulge the woman's wishes and become 'negligent of his skill and . . . use up all his wealth'. The merchant must guard against false love and desire for 'an infatuated heart is of no benefit'. Prostitutes should be avoided.

An important concern for any businessman was the hiring and management of staff, and the manuals gave valuable advice on this subject. The ideal situation was to have family members in key positions which enabled them to develop their capabilities. Nevertheless, a growing business will need to employ outside the family and the *Shanggu xingmi* stresses that a merchant should take great care when hiring servants. The background of each worker must be confirmed before taking them on. There is much danger in hiring someone with no background. As the slogan says, 'no root, not safe'[59]. But of course, the best option was for the worker to be of the same root, that is, the same family.

The manuals also advocated fair treatment of staff. For example, the *Dianye xuzhi* said that employers must give apprentices time off to visit their families. If a worker was given one or two months off, it would also show behaviour consistent with the Confucian focus on the family as the most important unit in society. The (*Shanggu xingmi*) advised employers not to be too heavy-handed when dealing with staff:

> If I supervise and regulate (the clerk), he will certainly not feel free. Resentment and anger will arise. His determination will slacken, and not only will he be unwilling to exert himself, he will also indulge his private desires and rejoice in my losses[60].

THE TRUE NATURE OF WEALTH

While business is conducted in pursuit of profit and wealth, the manuals reminded their readers to consider the true nature of wealth. A wealthy person was not one with a lot of money, but one with high morals. Businesses should consider this when making business decisions. For example, the *Shanggu xingmi* advises:

> . . . do not look at the money, but the actions that you did in order to earn it as the real wealth[61].

If a merchant was addicted to the pursuit of money, this would lead to a loss of righteousness. However, if a merchant made his money morally, his wealth and rank could be perceived as legitimate. The *Shishang leiyao* actually warns that if things are going badly for the merchant, it is because they are failing to act morally. Such warnings suggest that a merchant must act morally to avoid such pitfalls. There were certainly advantages to a business that gained a reputation for acting morally. The author of *Dianye xuzhi* came from Xinan, a region whose merchants were almost as successful as those from Huizhou. The author noted how these merchants were known for their honesty and sincerity, a reputation which enhanced their success[62].

If a businessman cultivated the virtue of honesty, it would give customers confidence to do business with them. By contrast, public criticism could prove fatal to one's reputation and business. Customers will not want to do business with you and your future income will suffer. It is better to retain customers. Also, if a business treats someone badly, they may be the target of revenge in the future. Consequently, a common theme is that the path to profit and riches is paved with moral behaviour.

Although the concept of 'happiness through doing good works' was common among successful merchants such as those from Huizhou, the handbooks did not deal much with charity. One that did was the *Shanggu xingmi*. With its strong basis in Confucian thought, this book advised merchants to engage in charity and share the benefits of commerce. A merchant should share the wealth and happiness that trade brought, rather than keep it to himself[63].

Consistent with the need to act morally and develop a good reputation, the manuals stressed the need to cultivate trust. For example, the *Maoyi xuzhi* stressed the need for transparency in price setting. Instead of simply increasing or decreasing prices, merchants can show that their pricing is fair by explaining to customers the reasons for any price change.

Another issue of importance to the cultivation of trust is the method by which payments are handled. Once again, the *Maoyi xuzhi* stresses transparency. When weighing silver or copper, it must be done in front of the customer. Similarly, counting coins or banknotes must be done in the customer's presence so as to remove any hint of fraud. Any excess money given in error must be returned:

> No matter whether it is coppers 'big' or 'small' silver coins or bank notes that are given you, they must be counted in front of the customer, so that you may not be suspected of fraud. You must be particularly careful about this when the sum is a large one[64].
>
> . . . if you are given too much, due to his error, you must return it. You will keep your innocence. You cannot take money that is not rightfully yours. There is an ancient saying 'to take this way is to be with manners'[65].

The manuals also gave practical advice on customer service. The advice reflects the standards of the time, so when a customer enters a shop, they should be greeted with cups of tea or a pipe for smoking. The customer should be allowed to take their time and be met with a 'kind and pleasant countenance'[66].

Although the manuals were written three hundred years after Marco Polo's visit, the superstition he observed still existed. Religious and superstitious acts permeated the business culture and found their way into merchant manuals. One particular aspect was the belief in auspicious days. Some days could be lucky or unlucky for conducting business. For example, the *Shanggu xingmi* identified sixty auspicious days that were lucky for trading, as well as identifying days when one should not trade or travel by boat[67].

Morality and religion were not the only guides to business behaviour. The manuals also advised merchants to respect the law. This included the need to adapt to local laws in the regions that merchants travelled to. It included the need to pay all taxes and not attempt to avoid customs duties. Manuals and route books went as far as explaining what the taxes were on different goods in each region.

Two final traits emphasised in the manuals were hard work and discipline[68]. Hard work was valued as it was this that generated a merchant's income. By contrast, laziness led to poverty. Discipline was important because it helped a merchant to avoid unnecessary trouble. Discipline could refer to restraint in expenditure, financial planning and decision making. It also referred to the management of one's family. A family member's ill-discipline can draw the whole family into unnecessary trouble and despair.

CHAPTER 8

The Qing Dynasty (1644–1911)

SUZHOU AND THE ART OF QING COMMERCE

China during the Qing dynasty was the largest national market economy in the world. Jesuit priests, who visited China in the seventeenth and eighteenth centuries, marvelled at the extent of the Chinese market:

> The inland trade of China is so great that the commerce of all Europe is not to be compared therewith; the provinces being like so many kingdoms, which communicate with each other their respective production[1].

There was one region of China that stood out above the others, so much so it could be described as the country's economic powerhouse. Jiangnan is an area slightly smaller than France, situated south of the lower Yangtze River. The region enjoyed its first period of economic pre-eminence during the Southern Song when China's capital was shifted to Hangzhou. This provided the first big stimulus to economic activity. However, when the Mongols shifted the capital back to the north, Jiangnan experienced a period of relative dormancy[2]. But in the late Ming and Qing dynasties, it experienced a renaissance that made it one of the wealthiest regions in the world.

The name 'Jiangnan' translates to 'south of the river'; however, the salt city Yangzhou, on the north bank of the Yangtze, is often included in its description[3]. It also includes the cities of Hangzhou and Suzhou, whose prosperity was legendary. A common saying compared these cities with heaven. It said, 'Above there is heaven; on earth, Suzhou and Hangzhou.'[4]

Jiangnan was the 'most prosperous and most highly urbanised region of the empire in the late imperial period'[5]. It set the pace for style throughout the empire. As one scholar wrote, 'what in Suzhou is considered elegant is considered elegant elsewhere, and everybody scorns what is scorned here as vulgar'[6].

The prosperity of this region has been captured in one of China's greatest works of art. In 1751, the emperor completed an inspection trip of the south, after which he commissioned the painting of a scroll from the court painter Xu Yang, who was a native of Suzhou. In 1759, Xu Yang completed the painting entitled *Prosperous Suzhou* (also known as *Burgeoning Life in a Resplendent Age*).

Twelve metres long, the scroll provides a view of everyday life in Suzhou, including a large range of business activities. We can see many examples of commerce in the Qing dynasty. It depicts numerous merchants, traders, shops and vendors. It includes shops selling furniture, a stand for dumplings and the entertainment industry with a theatrical performance. The transport industry is well represented with four hundred boats including barges and passenger boats carrying goods and people to the city.

Xu Yang's painting *Prosperous Suzhou* is a treasure not just for artists but for business historians, in capturing an efficient market and the high quality of living it supported. The prosperity he painted reflected a process that began during the Ming dynasty. This was a commercial centre par excellence with goods and services to meet the needs of the most discerning customer. A writer of the time noted, 'As for goods which are difficult to obtain in the four quarters (of the world), there are none which are not found here. Those who pass through are dazzled by its brilliance.'[7]

THE SOURCE OF SUZHOU'S PROSPERITY

The basis of Suzhou's wealth was its textile industry. In the Southern Song dynasty, Suzhou gained a reputation for the quality of its silk. This industry grew from the local geographic conditions. The region had a warm, humid climate with an abundance of water which was ideal for cultivating the silkworm. As with Jingdezhen's porcelain industry, the development of the market economy provided the opportunity to fully exploit the region's potential.

The practice of producing silk and rearing silkworms is known as sericulture. This process transforms the silkworm egg into fabric and involves a number of distinct processes. The initial phase involves cultivating mulberry for the worms to eat, raising silkworms and feeding them mulberry leaves. The raw silk comes from the worm's cocoons which must be carefully tended, after which it is reeled, wound, warped and woven into silk textiles[8]. Marco Polo had earlier told Europeans of his amazement at the silk industry based in Suzhou, saying:

> They have vast quantities of raw silk, and manufacture it, not only for their own consumption, all of them being clothed in dresses of silk, but also for other markets. There are amongst them some very rich merchants, and the number of inhabitants is so great as to be a subject of astonishment[9].

In the Yuan dynasty, the textile industry expanded to include cotton. Market development in the Ming dynasty helped the development of cotton production. As the industry grew, it provided jobs for many in the Jiangnan region who left their farms to gain employment in the city. There they gained new skills needed to participate in the industry, and a number of specialised capabilities diffused through the region including spinning, weaving, dyeing, calendering, tailoring, as well as the skills needed by transport and commercial workers[10]. In acquiring these skills, workers enhanced their income, meaning they had money to spend on other products and services. This process led to opportunities for businesses in other areas. For example, as the cotton-textile industry grew, it necessitated imports of raw cotton from other regions, stimulating economic activity in the regions that provided it[11].

The basic production unit in the textile industry was a *'jihu'*, which translates as 'textile family'. A textile firm was typically a family firm owning one or more looms. These formed the backbone of Suzhou's textile industry. Larger *jihu* that required additional labour might hire workers from outside the family.

Textile merchants played a vital role in the industry's operations, buying and selling supplies or finished product. This position meant they also played the prime role of organising and coordinating the different stages of production. Farmers might grow the initial crops (cotton, mulberry) but it was merchants who would carry their material to the towns where the next stage of production was performed. Merchants provided the spinners who created the yarn. They then bought the yarn and sold it to a weaver, whose output they would also buy and provide to a cloth wholesaler or retailer[12]. In so doing, they did not just supply goods or sell output, they were also setting the pace of production, coordinating resource flow with productive capabilities.

The industry was coordinated through a process of exchange. In the earlier Ming dynasty, Zhu Guozhen recorded how merchants sold supplies to producers who:

> Spin it into yarn or weave it into cloth. They go to the market early in the morning, exchange it for raw cotton, and then

return home where they again spin or weave it, taking it back the following morning to exchange[13].

The market was so dependable that households could rely entirely on their chosen specialised skill to survive[14]. Skilled workers had no trouble finding work. If they disliked their present working conditions, there was always another jihu to employ them. The size of the labour market also benefitted employers as workshops had no trouble finding skilled staff[15].

About this time, Suzhou witnessed the arrival of a new type of business. Large trading companies emerged to control the production process. In contrast to the organisation structure where a manufacturer controls the production process, these companies did no manufacturing. They were called 'accounting companies' but this name does not capture the full role they performed in regulating production. They provided raw material and commissioned work from the small workshops and independent craftsmen. They paid for the work and might provide tools. Then, when the work was finished, they would mark the finished product with their own brand, not that of the manufacturers. It is a system not too dissimilar to organisations today that subcontract production to other organisations. The accounting company handled the business side while the producers handled the manufacturing[16].

Textiles dominated Suzhou's economy with an estimated 50 to 60 per cent of men and women working by either spinning or weaving. On top of this were the merchants and other specialists. However, it was not the only industry in the city. At the end of the eighteenth century, there were more than thirty paper mills that collectively employed more than three hundred workers. Other manufacturers included shipyards, jade and jewellery workshops, metal and leather workshops and at least one hundred candle factories[17].

This output attracted merchants from all over China who came to buy textiles and other manufactured goods, at the same time as selling goods from their own regions. When combined with the high level of prosperity, Suzhou shops reflected a diversity unique in the world.

An example of the type of businessman who could thrive in such an environment is Sun Chunyang. He came from Ningbo where he received a Confucian education but failed in the examinations. He arrived in Suzhou at the end of the sixteenth century where he set up a small workshop situated in the city's trade quarters. He clearly had the skills to ride the growing market economy of the time, for his business grew to fill a huge bonded warehouse. It was located 'in a building that would have done a government office proud'[18].

Sun Chunyang developed his warehouse into six stores, each specialising in a particular type of product. These included salted meats, condiments, spices, sweets and candles. It included both Chinese and imported products. Contributing to this success was the quality of his products. Such was his reputation that his products became status symbols with commentators of the day boasting, for example, that they used Sun Chunyang's lamps and candles. The imperial household also bought products from his warehouse.

Sun Chunyang's management was also characterised by strong financial control. A tight financial management system was used. A customer entering the warehouse would pay a cashier and receive a receipt which they used to obtain the product of their choice. Each day, administrators finalised accounts which were tallied at the end of the year to form an annual total.

Tight financial management and quality products ensured this company's long life. One hundred and fifty years later, Qing dynasty writers were still exulting the efficiency and prosperity of the company[19].

THE SHANXI MERCHANT GROUP

The previous chapter described the key role that guilds played in promoting trust in the market. Merchant guilds were also known as business guilds or merchant groups. During the Ming and Qing dynasties (1368–1911), ten major merchant groups appeared with business links that spanned the empire. They may have started with merchants taking products from their home region to different parts of China. Initially they would have sold to middlemen in the distant towns, but as trade grew, the merchants might bypass the middlemen and establish their own permanent shops[20]. In this way trade networks were established that spanned the nation. However, as outsiders, they often had different dialects and customs to the locals and this exposed them to discrimination. Hence, they often formed guilds to provide each other support. For example, the rules of the Ningpo Merchants Association at Wen-chou-fu states:

> Here at Wenchow, we find ourselves isolated; mountains and sea separate us from Ningpo, and when in trade we excite envy on the part of the Wenchowese, and suffer insult and injury, we have no adequate redress. Mercantile firms, each caring only for itself, experience disgrace and loss – the natural outcome of isolated and individual resistance. It is this which imposes on us the duty of establishing a guild[21].

Merchant groups were characterised by their home region and ethnic linkages. We have already mentioned the success of the Huizhou Group. Equally prominent was the Shanxi Group. The Shanxi Group came to prominence in the early Ming dynasty when the government needed merchants to supply grain to military posts on the northern frontier. Many merchants from Shanxi gained commissions in this trade before moving on to the profitable salt trade. Like the Huizhou merchants, this enabled them to build significant wealth. It also enabled merchants to develop close contacts with government officials which further consolidated their position.

Shanxi was a province with abundant resources, and this provided a basis for many merchants to trade. Merchants could market raw resources or handicrafts made from those resources. They could be found all over China and were the most prominent merchants in many areas. For example, of Beijing it was said, 'Most of the rich merchants in Beijing come from Shanxi.' By the Qing dynasty, the Shanxi Merchant Group was recognised as one of the most powerful business forces in the country.

Shanxi merchants specialised in transportation by camel. The main commodity that they carried was tea. Their expertise in the distribution of tea included buying, processing, transporting and retail. They invested downstream and upstream, purchasing the mountain lands on which tea was grown and, at the other end of the market, they also owned tea franchise stores. They exported tea to Mongolia and Russia. Shanxi merchants also gained success in ocean shipping, transporting copper from Japan to China. However, the industry for which they are best known is banking.

The first Shanxi bank was established in 1823 by Li Daquan who owned a dyed goods operation that bought raw materials in Sichuan and operated stores in a number of distant centres including Beijing, Shenyang and Tianjin. A manager in Tianjin by the name of Lei Lutai noted how shipments of silver often passed each other, going in opposite directions[22]. Carrying silver on long journeys was danger-ous and incurred substantial security and transportation costs. A more effective method would be for each of the company's branches to retain their own cash, and a system of drafts would enable money to be drawn from each against the other branches without the need for shifting large volumes of cash.

The system was first introduced to address cash flowing between the various company's branches, but it became obvious that the service could be offered to other businesses. So Lei suggested to Li that he establish a bank that could act as a clearing house for such transactions. If a merchant decided, instead of carrying it, to put money in a bank in his hometown and withdraw it in the destination, it would eliminate these costs and money would no longer be shuffled to and fro.

Li founded the 'Rishengchang' which translates as the 'Sunrise Provident Bank' (*ri* – sun, *sheng* – rise, *chang* – prosperity). The banks were initially established in Tianjin, Wuhan and Pinyao. The new business was so lucrative that Li Daquan shifted his focus from dyed goods to branch banking, offering services in inter-regional accounts settlement, deposit accounts, loans, and currency exchange[23].

Lei served as general manager, with two assistant managers: Mao Hongsui and Cheng Dapei. However, after a few years, Mao and Lei disagreed over business strategy, so Mao quit to establish five banks of his own. Years later, some of his managers left his company to form their own banks. This pattern of industry growth has been observed today in modern business, whereby a manager gains experience and capabilities in an industry, and if operating in a growing market, leaves his employment to establish his own companies. For example, it has been seen in Silicon Valley where the company Silicon Fairchild performed a similar role to that of Li's Rishengchang bank in China.

The Shanxi banks quickly grew to build and dominate China's banking and financial industries. Within thirty years, eleven banks were established in Shanxi province, and by the end of the nineteenth century, thirty-two banks with 475 branches were spread throughout China[24].

THE CO-HONG

As wealthy as these merchants were, neither they nor the Huizhou merchants could match the wealth of a man from Canton, who in the early nineteenth century became the richest man in the world. He was a member of the Co-Hong, '*hong*' being the Cantonese variation on the word '*hang*' (guild). To Westerners, it is the most well known of all the Chinese guilds, its fame reflecting its function of trading with European companies coming to China. The records kept by the European trading companies meant a lot of information exists on the individual businessmen who ran these companies, their strategies and their personal characteristics.

China's pattern for dealing with foreign traders was established in the Tang dynasty when a superintendent of foreign trade was established to deal with sea-traders coming from as far as Arabia and Japan. Port regulations and customs collection procedures were established. The Chinese merchants who dealt with the foreigners were expected to help enforce government rules and duties. To maintain law and enable better surveillance, the foreigners were required to live in separate areas, grouped by nationality[25].

The mode of working with foreign seaborne traders established in the Tang dynasty became the pattern for dealing with foreigners since. There might be some modification, for example in the number of ports foreigners could visit, and there were times when foreign trade was completely outlawed. Within these provisos, the pattern of superintendent, foreign quarters and merchant participation in official requirements became the Chinese norm[26].

Europeans first started visiting China in 1513, when Portuguese explorers landed in Canton. It took some time for trade with Europe to become established because of the distance. For many years, the

Spanish and Dutch preferred to use their colonies in the Philippines and Indonesia as midway stations for the growing commerce.

In 1685, after a period of seclusion, the Qing government opened four ports to foreign trade. At the same time, French and British ships began visiting China in search of trading opportunities. The most exciting business opportunity appeared with a Chinese beverage: tea. The new traders carried the product back to Europe where customers quickly developed a taste for the drink. By 1732, Dutch, Swedish and Danish companies were also appearing in China with the goal of carrying tea to their home markets.

As in earlier times, the merchants were expected to co-operate with government officials in the management of this trade. However, the Qing dynasty was a time when the government was decreasing its involvement in commerce and delegating more to the guilds. Consequently the Co-Hong members found themselves responsible for collecting customs duties, monitoring the behaviour of foreigners, and other aspects of trade. In so doing, the entrepreneurs who entered this trade in search of profit became 'merchant bureaucrats'[27].

The merchants were not treated equally. Like the salt monopoly, there were different levels of merchants, so for example, in the 1720s, merchants were categorised into three different tiers depending on their wealth and ability. The top merchants were the Hong merchants who were given authority to 'secure' each visiting foreign ship. They were responsible for everything concerning the ship including trade, port fees, customs duties, crews and their activities[28]. The numbers in this group would change over time, but they came to be known as the 'thirteen hongs'.

Appointment of Hong merchants was decided by the local officials. This meant that the merchant's career was in their hands, so a merchant required a business strategy that included cultivating goodwill through gifts and fees[29]. The higher the ranking of the merchant, the more they were exposed to extortion by the officials. In such circumstances, the merchants were vulnerable as official disfavour was a worse fate than commercial failure. It could include imprisonment, confiscation of property, beatings and exile. Consequently, the chief merchant was also responsible for giving all the officials yearly gifts. The size of the gift depended on the ranking of the official. In 1757, the English estimated the value of these gifts at 20,000 *taels*[30].

Official extortion added a significant cost to the running of a business. When combined with the need to adapt to the changes in the trade, it helped contribute to a high rate of company dissolution. Fifteen businesses failed in the last quarter of the eighteenth century, with another eight in the first thirty years of the nineteenth century[31].

Initially, the numbers of foreign ships arriving in China was small. There might only be three or four ships arriving each year[32]. The trade was not big enough to develop specialist entrepreneurs devoted solely to the European trade. It attracted well-rounded merchants with investments in a number of areas including domestic trade and Chinese shipping, that is, the China Sea junk trade.

Of the four ports open to trade, the European companies tended to favour Canton in the south; consequently, many of the merchants from other regions found they had to move there in order to service the trade. Many of the earliest merchants came from Fujian where they already had experience in ocean-going trade. However, because of the small size of the trade, they would only stay temporarily in Canton. European sailing ships had to travel when the monsoon winds allowed. This meant they arrived in China around May or June, and departed by mid-January. This seasonal pattern allowed the merchants to return to their home province in the off-season.

The merchants might bring with them craftsmen, such as silk weavers who could quickly meet European orders. The European ships had a limited period of time in port and they needed to obtain a full shipload of products within that time. To ensure that there would be enough stock available, they would place orders for the next season, so that goods were ready when the ships arrived. If supplies could not be met locally, the Hong merchants placed orders with upcountry suppliers, who demanded advances to meet their costs. This put the merchant in a vulnerable position. If a merchant paid for the advance and a ship didn't arrive, it could destroy their business. To solve this problem, the foreign shippers took over payment of the advance, but this meant the whole system became dependent on foreign advances to operate[33].

Another peculiarity of the trade was the system referred to as 'truck'. Under this system, exports were tied to imports, so that if a merchant wanted to sell goods to a European trader, he was expected to buy imports from them. This could be a problem for the merchants, as their profits depended on their ability to sell the imported goods. In some cases, the European import might be highly marketable, such as tin, in which case the merchant might try to buy all the shipper's supply and gain control of the market. However, other products might have limited demand in China, leaving the merchant with hard-to-sell stock.

One problem with the truck system is that the ships generally arrived around the same time and flooded the market with imports, which then lowered the prices and profits. To counter this, merchants might store their stock until the market recovered, but warehousing tied up working capital, and most merchants could not afford to wait. They frequently had to sell goods at a loss to free up cash[34].

It is commonly believed that the Chinese did not sign contracts, but this is not true. Merchants did sign written contracts with foreigners and many of them still exist in the archives of the foreign trading companies[35]. It is true that they were not considered legal documents in China, but they helped to clarify the obligations of each party, and magistrates would refer to them when settling disagreements.

Contracts could vary in their terms and reflected the peculiarities of the trade and the strategy of any given merchant. Chinese merchants were very flexible and produced a diverse range of contracts[36]. They needed to make the most of the resources available to them at any given time. For example, on one occasion a Danish ship arrived with insufficient funds to pay an advance for a supply of tea. This meant the merchant had to pay the advance to his suppliers, or find an alternative source of cash which would require paying interest. To accommodate this, the Danes were charged a price 20 per cent higher than the market rate for tea.

To work at this level of flexibility required strong business skills. For the Danish example above, working out a fair rate of interest required knowledge of the value of money over time. They also needed to be aware of exchange-rate fluctuations, and if silver was paid, whether the silver was of consistent quality.

Merchants also needed to pay attention to their product quality and underlying processes. Foreign companies were very sensitive to quality and demanded reimbursement if the product was below par. Consider the packing of tea. If the merchant packed a lot of tea in each chest, it maximised the use of cargo space; however, it could lead to crushed leaves and tea dust at the bottom of the chest. If the tea was packed on a hot day, it might get contaminated with the perspiration of the coolie who packed the chest. On the other hand, if packed on a rainy day, moisture could get into the chest and spoil the product.

In 1755, the European preference for Canton became official, as the Chinese government made it the sole port open to foreign trade. This gave the Canton Co-Hong a monopoly when dealing with the

Europeans, although there was still competition between the merchants. In 1757, there were twenty-six Chinese firms licensed for foreign trade in the port. Half of these had the rights to deal with foreigners, six of which were given first-tier status as 'capital merchants' with significant regulatory powers. The other thirteen had limited rights: dealings in foreign goods without the right to secure ships nor ship goods abroad[37].

By the middle of the eighteenth century, more ships were arriving in China with larger orders for Chinese exports. This required a new type of merchant, a specialist who could devote himself solely to trade with Europeans. This was a period when many of the old merchants withdrew from the business and a number of new entrants appeared. The new merchants were dealing with larger orders so, instead of meeting their orders from local craftsmen, they became increasingly reliant on suppliers from upcountry. However, this increased the financial demands on the merchants who not only needed to finance the purchase of larger orders, but also had to provide part payment in advance. As a consequence, they found themselves in a perpetual state of debt.

This state of indebtedness could have been solved if they had been able to use the new forms of equity finance that businesses in Europe and North America had access to. Equity finance involved shareholders buying shares of a business for the long term. Shareholders are only paid a dividend if the company makes a profit, in which case the company does not need to pay out in a bad year. By contrast, a loan requires interest payments no matter how bad the returns are, and this makes it hard to survive the bad times. Equity finance options were very limited in China, a reflection that Chinese business methods were now falling behind those in the West.

Another problem contributing to their financial woes was the poor saleability of the products that Europeans brought to trade.

European products did not arouse the level of consumer interest in China that silks, porcelain and tea did in Europe. One can only wonder whether, if Chinese merchants arrived in Europe, they might have done a better job at identifying potential imports given their better knowledge of the Chinese consumer.

The first major business failure was that of Beaukeequa. Like many of the merchants of the time, he originated from Quanzhou in Fujian, but traded in Canton between 1726 and 1734. He first appears in European records in January 1727, when he is recorded selling a thousand pieces of silk to the Ostend General India Company. He appears to be a specialist in silk, employing his own weavers who he brought with him from Fujian. He gained a reputation for the quality of his product which enabled him to charge high prices, as the statement from a European in 1732 accords:

> Beau Keyqua had the Character of making the best silks of any Body here though dearer, yet as the difference of the Goodness would easily make amends for that if not too great, I thought of buying some of him. But . . . He not only kept the price up very high but also fairly told me that he could not promise to have them ready in less than 110 days, which I saw was making a jest of us. Since no body to ask more than 70 or 80 days at the longest, as soon as I gave over thinking more of him[38].

By 1732, he was recognised as one of the pre-eminent merchants in Canton, supplying silks to the English, Dutch and French, but his trade was not limited to Europeans. He also invested in the junk trade sailing to South East Asia where he appeared to sell his stock for gold. However, in 1733, the English reported that he had fallen out of favour with the mandarins, for reasons we are not aware of. They noted:

1733, Dec 5: Beau Khiqua we believe to be a person of substance . . . but being obliged to decline trade this year, on account of some disgust the Mandareens have taken to him, we did but little business with him[39].

Beaukeequa returned to his home in Fujian where he stayed for fifteen years. We know little about him in that time, but in 1748 he returned to Canton at a time when a number of other merchants were making the same migration. However, this time he had a new strategy. He was determined to grow his business as fast and large as possible[40]. He traded in porcelain and tea, and also made significant investments in Canton property. To enable this, he relied on debt financing. Such a strategy relies on gaining a rapid increase in profit that enables the merchant to pay off debt and build up assets.

On 11 September 1758, Beaukeequa suddenly died. His death revealed the true state of his business. He did not have enough assets or income to cover his liabilities. We do not know the reason for this failure. The English blamed his fall on excessive 'squeezing' by the local officials and problems with secret contracts he had with European companies. One thing for sure is that high debt strategies leave businesses highly vulnerable to negative circumstances. For example, if a ship fails to arrive in port when expected, the loss of income will hurt all merchants, but for a merchant heavily in debt, it can be disastrous. His high growth/high debt strategy was always risky.

The Richest Man in the World

At the end of the eighteenth century, the trade changed once again, with the arrival of country ships. Up until this time, European ships had been operated by chartered companies like the English East India Company, which had been given a monopoly by their home governments. But the late eighteenth century saw the arrival of many smaller companies. These companies did not have the same financial clout and stability of the great East India companies. Nor did they purchase supplies in the same quantity. Nevertheless, they were a significant and growing part of the trade, which once again required a change in the capabilities of the Chinese merchants. There were more orders, but each order was smaller. Most important, the country traders brought imports with them that needed to be sold and this placed an emphasis on the merchants' selling skills[41]. A merchant left with a load of unsellable stock faced serious financial problems.

One product brought by the country traders that dramatically changed the nature of the trade was opium. The English East India Company supplied the opium in India where they held auctions at which country traders purchased their supplies. The country traders then transported the drug to China. This rise in trafficking led the Chinese government to issue an edict against its importation in 1799, which was repeated again in 1807 and 1809[42]. At that time, about four thousand crates of opium were arriving each year.

By 1830, the figure had climbed to 14,000 crates, five thousand of which came from one country trader, Jardines[43]. Despite the edicts, the opium trade was tolerated because it increased the level of legal trade. Chinese merchants paid for the opium in silver, which the foreigners then used to purchase legal Chinese goods. This increased the overall level of trade, which in turn increased business for suppliers inland as well as raising income for the state. Consequently, the senior officials turned a blind eye to the trade[44].

By 1836–7, the Co-Hong were responsible for fifty-five foreign firms and 307 resident foreigners, whose business included over two hundred foreign ships with total tonnage of more than 100,000[45]. Export duties yielded the government between 4 million and 4.5 million taels annually. Not only was this a welcome boost to government coffers but it provided jobs for many Chinese in the tea, silk and porcelain industries, as well as those engaged directly in the opium trade.

The merchant who profited most from trading with Westerners was Howqua, although it is uncertain to what extent he traded in opium. Howqua is on public record as being opposed to the opium trade; however, his American business partners included Perkins & Co, and Russell & Co who were active in the trade[46].

Howqua was descended from a respectable family of Fujian merchants. His grandfather moved to Canton early in the eighteenth century, along with others who migrated at the time. His family originated from a region producing black tea, a product with which Howqua would build a fortune by selling it to Europeans and Americans.

His father, Howqua I, had been the purser for one of the leading merchants in the Co-Hong, Phuankhequa, before establishing his own business. European records reveal that in 1769 his father was contracting in his own name. In 1801, Howqua II took over the family business and quickly established himself as a man of unique ability. He held the position of chief merchant in the Hong from 1811 to 1815, and 1822 to 1842.

Those he dealt with consistently praised both his business skills and his character. His obituary notes how his 'knowledge and even familiarity with mercantile details connected with the trade of foreign ports were truly astonishing; sound judgement; true prudence, wary circumspection, and a wise economy were distinguishing traits of his mercantile character'[47]. If there was one aspect of his character they were critical of, it was his timidity in the face of government officials. His obituary noted that the 'local mandarins, and perhaps also some at Pekin(g), were well aware that Howqua was made of squeezable materials'[48].

Howqua formed a close relationship with American traders. The first American ship to sail to China was the 360-ton *Empress of China*.

It was owned by a syndicate of Philadelphia merchants including Robert Morris, who had helped finance the American Revolution and signed the Declaration of Independence. The first voyage generated a 25 per cent profit of $30,000 for the Americans, from a cargo of porcelain, silk pieces and other Chinese goods. (By way of comparison, an annual income of $2,000 would have kept a family of gentle folk in comfort.)[49]

Americans tried selling a number of products to the Chinese, including furs and iron, but sales only covered 35 per cent of the goods coming the other way[50]. This meant they had to pay cash for the balance. Many of the new American companies formed business relationships with Howqua who valued the influx of silver. He became their prime, if not sole supplier of tea[51]. Their relationship lasted many decades until his death.

American companies also entered the opium trade; however, they were not able to get their supplies from India, which was the domain of the British East India Company and their associated private traders. The Americans found their supply in Turkey, from the port of Smyrna[52]. American merchants involved in the trade included Astor, Girard, Perkins & Co, Russell & Co, John Donnell of Baltimore and Joseph Peabody of Salem.

In the 1830s, an incident occurred which says much about the character of Howqua and the relationship he had with the Americans. At that time, the American-owned Russell & Co experienced financial problems brought on by a crash in the London finance markets. Howqua came to the rescue of his American friends. He wrote to the firm's bankers, Barings & Co, telling them that he would send money to cover any outstanding bills drawn by Russell & Co, if the Americans could not do so themselves. This gesture saved the American company from bankruptcy.

Such was their gratitude that in 1844, an American tea trader A. A. Low, named a new ship *Howqua* after the great merchant.

A portrait of Howqua hangs in a Salem museum today as a reminder of the gratitude that the Americans felt towards him. Westerners consistently praised his character. He was known to be honest, friendly and generous, and this did not stop him from making a fortune. By the time of his death, at the age of seventy-five, his fortune was believed to be at least $25 million, making him the richest man in the world at the time.

CHAPTER 9

Overseas Chinese in South East Asia

·············

In 1995, the Australian government published a report on ethnic Chinese living outside of China, in South East Asia. The report noted that those Chinese were much richer than those living in China:

> The 50 million or so ethnic Chinese resident in East Asia outside China generate an estimated GDP equivalent of about US$450 billion. This is almost on a par with China's GDP of approximately US$500 billion which is generated by more than 20 times in number of people.[1]

The fact that foreign-domiciled Chinese were producing twenty times as much as those in China would suggest that the Chinese business environment was holding people back from reaching their true potential. They did much better when they lived in other environments. However, the report also found that those living in South East Asia did much better than other ethnic groups living in the same environment:

> Although they are fewer than 10% of the population of South East Asia, ethnic Chinese make up 86% of its billionaires. They control much of the region's non land capital and its retail trade, and are major stakeholders in most of the region's economies.[2]

This suggests that it is not just the environment – so what is it that makes these people so rich? A common answer to this question is to assume that these rich Chinese are descendants of early traders who settled in South East Asia centuries ago, and have over time traded themselves to wealth. However, this explanation has limited support, as will be explained.

EARLY OFFSHORE COMMUNITIES

Chinese traders have been sailing to South East Asia since the Song dynasty. This was a time when the region was ruled by native princes. Traders and artisans settled abroad as agents for their family businesses, setting up bases in the ports, mines and cities where profit could be made. By the early fifteenth century, a number of Chinese communities were scattered throughout the region.

Merchant networks were established in the same way that Huizhou traders established networks within China, the only difference being that these were international and they were primarily from Fujian province which was the base for trade to south Asia. The merchants, mostly men, normally returned to China but some married local women, settled down and brought up their families. One would suspect that these early settlers provided a good basis for building great fortunes. However, over time, the descendants became so assimilated with the local populations that they lost their Chinese nature.

These offshore traders settled in small groups throughout east Asia, but in two locations they established large communities. These were at Manila in the Philippines and Batavia in Indonesia. In the sixteenth century, the Spanish had seized control of the Philippines. It was the destination point for the famed Manila Galleons that carried silver across the Pacific from South America. This trade was of benefit to both the Spanish and Chinese. To build

Manila as an important commercial centre, the Spanish relied on Chinese ships, traders and artisans who migrated there in large numbers. They welcomed the Chinese who enjoyed the new commercial opportunities the Spanish had created. Chinese traders flocked to Manila where they traded goods for the Spanish silver. As early as the 1580s, twenty ships a year were coming from Fujian carrying silks, porcelains, food, furniture and other manufactured goods.

The Chinese did not just come as traders. They also came as artisans and builders and by 1603, some 25,000 were living in Manila, making it the first large-scale overseas Chinese community[3]. As was normal for the time, a distinct area was created for the foreigners, the Parian. However, cross-cultural interaction is fraught with difficulty, and a trip to the Philippines by Chinese officials proved the catalyst for disaster.

A man by the name of Tio Heng had told the emperor that the Philippines possessed an exceptionally rich mountain producing enormous amounts of gold and silver. So an official entourage was sent to the Philippines to confirm whether this was true. The Spanish rulers looked at this deputation with great anxiety. They were suspicious about the true nature of the visit, and began wondering if it might be the precursor to a Chinese invasion. Their anxieties grew further when the officials started administering justice to local Chinese. It was not their job to administer justice in the Spanish Philippines.

The visiting mandarins soon discovered there was no gold and silver mountain, and on return to China recommended discipline for the men who had deceived and humiliated them. Some officials had thought the trip could cause trouble and they were right. The visit had stirred up a climate of distrust between the two populations. The Spanish were very anxious that an invasion might follow, and started strengthening defences and placing restrictions on the local Chinese. Observing these changes, the local Chinese thought the Spanish were preparing to kill them. They responded by rebelling, which soon turned into a localised battle and a massacre of 23,000 Chinese[4].

The Chinese population was annihilated, but soon new traders and artisans arrived and by 1621, the numbers had risen again to over twenty thousand. Some of these were temporary residents who later returned to China, but many stayed, some converting to Catholicism. Just as in China, the sojourning communities lived in groups based on their trade, clan, village or county origins. The Spanish gave the Chinese freedom to organise themselves as they chose. Chinese merchants set up wholesale and retail businesses around the country, often as part of an import/exporting network. If they needed anything from officials they found that a bribe was sufficient to obtain the desired outcome, a practice similar to the giving of gifts to officials in Canton.

Cultural challenges were always present for the offshore Chinese merchants. In the new environments, they had to learn new languages, laws and customs. They might also be exposed to racial discrimination or political intrigue, but the Chinese adapted to the environment as circumstances dictated[5]. In Thailand or any region run by native rulers, they found that the goods they sold were highly desired, and this placed them in a strong position when it came to bargaining. Sometimes the merchants developed strong connections with the rulers, achieving high positions in the government or perhaps becoming the ruler's merchant-representative.

When the Chinese dealt with Dutch or British colonists, a different approach was needed. The cultural differences were greater and commercial activities were more likely governed by rules and regulations rather than political whim. They also found that Western officials, unlike the mandarins back home, recognised the importance of profit, and recognised the Chinese as talented traders. Hence, in some foreign locations, they gained a 'freedom to develop their talents and expand their business empires in ways unknown in Chinese history'[6].

The Chinese prospered under a legal environment that supported commerce. This can be seen in the statement below by the Malaysian prime minister, Mahathir bin Mohamad, who described how:

> In no time at all, perfect 'rapport' was established between the Chinese traders and the conquering merchants of the West. As this partnership grew and as the Chinese partners proved their usefulness over and over again, Chinese migration to Malaysia speeded up.[7]

With the exception of Manila and Batavia, the overseas Chinese communities in South East Asia were not large but, in the nineteenth century, a new wave of migration occurred. This wave has been described as the Coolie Pattern of migration in which large numbers of poor coolie labourers left China in search of their fortune. The best-known examples of these occurred with the gold rushes in North America and Australasia, but it also included migration to find jobs on plantations or building railways. This was a transitory form of migration and most Chinese returned home at the end of their contracts.[8]

It was the next wave of migration that provided the existing group of billionaires, although they had similarly poor origins. Between 1870 and 1940, a number of countries needed labour to complete development projects, so once again large numbers of Chinese coolies left China to work in the jobs popping up in the ports and towns of South East Asia. They provided labour for the docks, saw mills, rice mills and construction industries.

The British were particularly active in recruiting Chinese to their colonies in Malacca, Penang and Singapore. The vast majority of the migrants came from the southern coastal provinces of Guangdong (Canton), Fujian and Hainan. They were leaving behind a China that was no longer wealthy and offered few opportunities. The late Qing dynasty was marred by famines and rebellions, so migrants sailed away with hope of fortune for their families. For many, their dreams came true. In fact, so successful were they that their descendants often faced government regulations to reduce the gap in wealth between them and other ethnic groups. Somehow these poor coolie labourers transformed themselves into wealthy businessmen. How did they do it?

How Did They Become So Successful?

Victor Limlingan was an academic at the Asian Institute of Management before commencing his own successful business career. In 1985, he released a study on the business strategies of overseas Chinese[9]. His observations provide some important insights into how these businesses succeeded.

Limlingan explained that when offshore Chinese first started businesses, their initial strategy was one of cost leadership. This was the logical strategy for a group that was characterised by cheap labour. By employing other coolies, normally family members, they could keep their costs low. But cheap labour was not the only factor that enabled them to keep prices low. They also took a low profit margin on each product they sold. This low margin was compensated by the large number of products they would sell. It was a high volume/low margin strategy.

In 1982, a comparison was published of financial statistics of Chinese firms and non-Chinese firms operating in the Philippines[10]. The asset turnover figure tells us that the Chinese did indeed have a higher volume of turnover, 4.8 compared to 1.82 for non-Chinese, and as expected their gross margin was much smaller. This illustrated the higher sales and turnover of stock that compensated for a lower profit on each individual sale.

	Chinese	Non-Chinese
Asset turnover	4.08	1.82
Debt leverage (debt/equity)	2.99	2.27
Gross margin on sales	9.1%	14.1
Gross profit/equity	148.04	83.99
ROE (net income/equity)	14.61	16.79

An interesting point from these figures is their higher debt leverage. The Chinese were more likely to finance their business through credit and loans, rather than investing equity into the business. This helps to identify another source of competitive advantage that the Chinese had.

To understand Chinese methods of financing, we need to describe Chinese social organisation. These groups could take the form of Chambers of Commerce, voluntary associations or clan groups. These groups act in the same way that guilds worked in China. They collected money for charities, settled business disputes, and represented the group's interests when dealing with government officials. However, these groups also acted as vehicles for information on market conditions and creditworthiness.

The community groups were arenas in which businessmen's transactions were observed by others. At meetings, these dealings were exposed to gossip and the scrutiny of others in the group. All members knew that others would be discussing their activities, just as they too would gossip about other members. It placed huge pressure on a businessman to uphold his reputation for trust and business acumen. It was also an effective method for assessing creditworthiness, and as a consequence, affected the rates of interest that Chinese merchants had to pay. One study of merchants in

Vietnam found that Chinese merchants paid interest rates of 2 to 3 per cent per month compared to 4 to 6 per cent for Vietnamese traders[11]. Lower interest rates added to their competitiveness and ability to charge low prices. It also provided an incentive to rely on credit/loan finance.

The importance of social groups and business networks was even more pronounced given the nature of the business environment in which they operated. South East Asia was characterised by developing nations with poor information and inadequate transport. In such an environment, the networks were an important business asset that compensated for the weaknesses in the environment. They were forums for discussion providing valuable information about trade conditions. If a gap in the market opened, the groups were a source of information on its occurrence. The groups also helped entrepreneurs seize opportunities. The merchants knew who they could approach to raise capital, and those lending money knew who they could trust. Because of the efficiency of this information, a businessman could raise capital quickly and cheaply. They did not need to go to a lawyer or bank, and incur all the associated transaction costs.

Not needing to incur these transaction costs provided cost advantages, and also enabled the Chinese businessman to act quickly. Through their networks, they could mobilise capital rapidly and channel it into high-profit opportunities. However, businessmen knew that they must succeed, for the eyes of the community were on them and, if they failed, they would not have the same access to resources next time. In this way, the network acted as a powerful enforcement mechanism for trust and high business performance.

Such were the subtleties of these networks, it has been said that the dialect spoken determines who a Chinaman does business with. They preferred doing business within their own group; however, they would at times do business with other Chinese and non-Chinese. The fact that Chinese communities were a minority in these countries meant they had no choice but to do business with other ethnicities.

If they were doing business with outsiders, they could not rely on the same information flows so had to use different methods. Victor Limlingan explains one technique that Chinese use when assessing the creditworthiness of people outside their ethnic group. It is based on the premise 'that any businessman worth his salt should have some access to cash, the only question being its cost'[12]. So, if a businessman wishes to buy goods but asks for credit, Chinese businessmen commonly refuse the credit but make a counter offer for a cash discount. In which case, a creditworthy businessman would be able to use the money saved from the discount to pay interest on a loan to pay for the goods. For example:

> ... if a non-Chinese businessmen were to ask for a 30 day credit on a specific purchase, a Chinese supplier may make a counter offer of a 5 percent cash discount. If the non-Chinese insists on the created extension despite this offer, then the Chinese businessmen rightly concludes that the non-Chinese businessmen has no access to credit that charges a maximum of 5% per month ... If the non-Chinese businessmen is readily able to come up with the cash then his access to cash is proven and will probably be extended credit the next time.[13]

Putting One's Money to Work

Limlingan describes the Chinese businesses as deal-makers[14]. The business outlook was primarily one of deal making, and sophisticated businessmen can be involved in several deals at any given time. Some deals might be ongoing while others might be one-off ventures. It was common for a Chinese trading company to be involved in ongoing activities, for example acting as an established distributer of products to rural areas, or buying commodities from farmers, then processing and transporting them to the urban centres. These long-term activities provided the basis on which other deals could be made. That is, they provided revenue with which other deals could be made, and they provided information when other opportunities popped up. An example of such an opportunity might be a building project which needed supplies in a hurry. A merchant would hear of the project through his contacts and have formed a supply-contract long before the news reached others.

The problem with short-term opportunities is that they pop up unexpectedly, in which case they cannot be programmed for, so a merchant needs to be prepared to act at short notice. Such opportunities require immediate decision, immediate action and funding. It also requires the ability to assess whether the deal is worth pursuing or not, in order to screen out the good deals from the bad ones. Not only does this require analysis skills, but also knowledge of the activity, and negotiations skills to ensure the terms of the deal are favourable.

A common question a businessman asks when discussing a deal is, 'How long will the money sleep?' When a businessman makes a deal, cash is invested, at which point it is perceived as going to sleep. It does not wake up again until he receives his cash back, hopefully growing bigger during the slumber. So for example, if cash is used to buy stock, it does not wake up until the goods have been sold and paid for, at which point it can be used for another deal.

This approach means the Chinese are particularly attuned to cash flow, a feature that has led to the downfall of many Western businesses. They have a particular focus on the cash generation cycle and the benefits of fast turnover. A number of techniques are used to maximise cash flow. This includes deferring payment to suppliers for as long as possible (without damaging the relationship), being prepared to dump inventory at a loss, and offering discounts to encourage quick cash payments.

They can be very imaginative in the way they maximise access to cash through deals. For example, imagine a tyre manufacturer is selling tyres by offering three months' credit before payment is due. A Chinese businessman might buy $200,000 of these tyres then sell them at $195,000. At first this seems poor business as he has lost $5,000. However, the $195,000 coming in can be used for other business deals during the credit period, that pay enough to cover the $5,000 as well as providing additional income.

CHANGING BUSINESS MODELS

South East Asia was characterised by markets with low-income consumers. Hence it made sense for the Chinese to offer products with cheap prices. They could do this because they had access to low-interest loans and were prepared to accept low profit margins on each sale. By successfully competing in this market, they removed less efficient competitors, effectively clearing the market of non-Chinese competition.

This pattern of business enabled the Chinese to develop profitable businesses, but there is a limit to which this strategy can be applied. Many companies reached a point where, if they wanted further growth, they would have to change their business model. The need to change was particularly pronounced because of changes in the business environment that were undermining the traditional low-cost model. In particular, the advantage of low-cost labour was being undermined when other firms used Indian migrants and Javanese workers. Secondly, many governments introduced labour reforms to end abuses occurring to the coolie workers. This had the effect of raising Chinese costs.

These changes forced the Chinese trading companies to modify their business model. Victor Limlingan noted that if a trader wished to build on his existing business, he had a number of options to choose from. They were:

1. Integrate forward into the distribution system (from dealer to mass merchandiser)
2. Integrate backward into the distribution system
3. Integrate backward into production
4. Expand into other product lines
5. Diversify into other business activities[15]

The first option of integrating forward enables traders to increase the volume of their business transactions and benefit from economies of scale. This might include warehousing, in-house transportation or processing (e.g. rice milling). It has proven popular with traders operating in big cities who have invested in mass merchandising and built superior retail outlets such as the Central Department Store in Bangkok and the Makati Supermarket in Manila.

The second option of integrating backward into the distribution system can be dangerous as it brings them into competition with big producers who are already competing at that end of the market. Consequently, Limlingan says that only the sharpest of traders choose and succeed in this option. The problem with integrating back into production is that the activities involved are often very different to that in which the trader excels. For example, if he integrates backward into rice farming, the trader must compete in terms of production efficiency, not trading proficiency. He cannot exploit his existing sources of competitive advantage.

The strategy chosen must be one which allows the business to apply their competitive advantage otherwise, by definition, they will have trouble competing. For this reason, not many firms pursued a strategy of diversification. If they did diversify, it was normally into areas like transportation and financing.

The best strategy builds on the trader's existing strengths and, for that reason, they are most likely to expand into new products that appeal to their existing market. In which case, they can generate additional revenue without incurring new marketing or transportation costs. In fact, it enables the trader to exploit more fully their existing set-up, for example getting more use from their trucks. This is a classic example of 'economies of scope' in which greater efficiency is gained by expanding product offerings into areas compatible with the existing business structure. The alternative, of course, is 'economies of scale' in which a business does more of the same and experiences cost decreases as output grows. However, this strategy is limited by the size of the market.

Expanding the range of products and supplies offers other important advantages. Given the Chinese use of credit as a source of finance, a new supplier also represents a source of credit, thereby increasing the company's resource base.

The choice of strategy is strongly dependent on the environment in which a business operates, and, in the 1950s, governments throughout South East Asia introduced policies which would strongly influence the direction of Chinese businesses. Some of these policies were highly discriminatory against the overseas Chinese. For example, when the Philippines gained independence from the United States in 1946, they introduced a Filipino first policy which restricted Chinese commercial activity in foreign exchange, trading and agriculture[16]. Similarly, in Indonesia, Chinese were prohibited from owning certain businesses, forced out of some things, like rice milling, altogether.

The Malaysian government did not force the Chinese to divest any of their activities but introduced a very strong form of 'positive discrimination' for Bumiputras (Malays) that limited future opportunities for Chinese. The goal of this policy was to create a society where all members contributed equally to the socio-economic development of the country.

These policies were clearly unfair to Chinese merchants who had worked hard and developed successful business practices.

However, it could be argued that these policies were motivated by the same goals as the Confucian policies that had often restricted businesses in China, that is, the desire to achieve social harmony. In fact, it could be claimed they were much softer than the Chinese policies in that they aimed for equality, whereas the Chinese policies actually aimed to put merchants on the lowest rung of the social ladder. Confucianism sought to reinforce a rigid social hierarchy. Nevertheless, just because the traditional Chinese policies were worse does not ease the pain. Most people in their position would rightly feel aggrieved.

While these policies were aimed at reducing social inequalities, other policies introduced at the time were devoted to stimulate national economic growth. These policies opened up new opportunities for the Chinese. In Malaysia and Thailand, economic growth policies were designed to develop their nation's agricultural base. However, in Indonesia and the Philippines, their economic development plans sought to industrialise their economies through import substitution.

To help stimulate industrial development, the Indonesian government protected local industries with high tariff rates, granted business monopolies in some markets, provided generous credit, tax breaks and government guarantees, and exempted businesses from some government regulations. These industrial shelters offered huge possibilities to anyone who could develop a business in a targeted industry, or bribe the government to obtain a monopoly or similar protection. With their wealth, the Chinese were well placed to do this. Many Chinese started businesses in these new industries, and achieved high profits because the government protected them from more efficient competitors.

Protected by high tariffs, market monopolies and government subsidies, the local Chinese firms flourished without any need to modernise their business and management structures. With no competition, there was little pressure to increase efficiency. If, however, they needed new expertise or technology, government policies enabled them to form joint ventures with foreign investors.

The Philippine economic development policy was very similar to that in Indonesia. It, too, pursued an industrialization policy based on import substitution, and the Chinese living there also responded by investing in manufacturing, particularly in textiles, hardware, final processing and assembling. The protection from efficient external competition enabled some Chinese to make large fortunes.

The individual strategies pursued by Chinese businesses were developed in response to the government policies and the changing business environment. They varied from country to country. The industrial policies in Indonesia and the Philippines supported diversification into new areas. In Thailand, where agriculture was targeted by the government, the Chinese were more likely to invest in this sector. In Malaysia, political strategies became important to ensure the Bumiputra policy did not detrimentally affect their position. In Singapore, businessmen responded to government signals and policies that sought to develop the nation as a regional trading and financial centre. In this way, the policies prompted the Chinese throughout South East Asia to invest in new activities that they previously had limited exposure to.

Liem Sioe Liong and His Salim Group

An example of one of the most successful businessmen in South East Asia was Liem Sioe Liong. Born in 1916 in China's Fujian province, he emigrated to Indonesia in 1936 and settled in the central Java town, Kundus. Here, he worked in his uncle's peanut trading business and, after ten years, branched out on his own trading in cloves. Like many Chinese traders before him, he bought his stock directly from the farmers then sold it to clove cigarette producers. In this way, he was performing the same middleman role that Chinese merchants in the Song dynasty performed.

During this time, Liem built up one of the most important business assets: personal connections. Indonesia at the time was still a Dutch colony and, in the era of independence, Liem became the supplier to a newly established division of the Indonesian army, trading clothing, medicine, food and medical supplies. The connections formed at this time would be of great use in the future. The quartermaster was Suharto, who later became the country's president.

In 1952, Liem moved to Jakarta, establishing an import/export business. He also entered a phase of expansion based on investment in manufacturing. As stated earlier, the new Indonesian government introduced policies that discriminated against Chinese traders, so the move from trading to manufacturing was a response to environment change. Liem invested in the manufacture of textiles, nails and bicycle parts. He also established a soap factory, drawing on his previous contacts to be supplier to the Indonesian armed forces.

Liem's fortunes improved dramatically when the government collapsed and General Suharto came to power. Together with another company, Liem was given a monopoly on importing cloves. Although Indonesia grew cloves, there were times when domestic clove production needed to be supplemented with imports. This was a substantial and highly profitable monopoly on which Liem's company was guaranteed a 5 per cent commission.

He also received a monopoly for flour and established the Bogasari Flour Mills. From this base, he then invested in a number of related businesses including the production of flour bags and bulk shipping to transport wheat to Indonesia from Australia, Canada and the United States. These businesses provided significant capital with which he could invest in other industries including cement and food manufacturing.

On one occasion, President Suharto was asked to justify this preferential treatment given to Liem's companies in food (Indofood) and cement (Indocement), and he responded by stressing his economic development goals, saying, 'The development of these two companies is not a collusion between me and Oom Liem, but the government's effort to reach self-sufficiency by utilising a businessman who is willing to work.'[17]

Liem's strategies for the Salim group at the time became the complete opposite of the pioneering Chinese entrepreneurs who focused on low cost. By reducing costs, those entrepreneurs ensured the consumer got excellent value for money. However, the Salim group kept prices high through its monopoly power. One study found that the flour mills charged three times the world price at the time.[18] Unsurprisingly, the Salim group was attracted to businesses in which it could achieve significant market power.

Not only can market domination be attained through political links but also by working in co-operation with other major firms; it was a strategy that became common with prominent ethnic Chinese companies in South East Asia. For example, in 1994, the Salim group purchased a stake in Malaysia's Kuantan Flour mills. This complemented the investments of another South East Asian billionaire, Robert Kuok, who had large flour milling interests in Malaysia. Liem and Robert Kuok were partners in many ventures across Asia. Their joint activities allowed them to share information and generate higher than normal returns[19].

The Salim group now operates throughout the world. In 2004, *Forbes* magazine listed Liem as the twenty-fifth richest man in South East Asia with a fortune of $655 million. Like the salt merchants in China, Liem gained significant wealth from his relationship with the government and the awarding of a monopoly[20].

CHINESE BUSINESSES IN INDIA

Clearly Liem was one of the stars of the overseas Chinese, and not all Chinese have the good fortune of forming contacts with someone who later becomes the president, nor the wealth to gain monopolies by giving to the ruling elite. While we are interested in the very rich, we are also interested in those who have succeeded at a lower level. Professor Ellen Oxfeld from Middlebury College studied one such group: the Chinese who immigrated to Calcutta, India, and rose to dominate the local tannery industry[21].

The earliest record of Chinese migration to Calcutta is that of a sailor who arrived in the 1770s. The sailor, known as Atchew or Acchi, apparently sailed from Guangdong (Canton) in a British ship. It is believed that the British Governor of Bengal, Warren Hastings, offered Atchew as much land as he could cover on horseback in a day, not knowing that Atchew was an expert rider. Consequently, Atchew gained a great deal of land from the agreement. He then brought in Chinese workers as indentured labourers to grow sugar cane on the land.

However, it seems that some of the labourers failed to fulfil their contract and ran away, for in 1781, Atchew wrote to Warren Hastings to help return them. As with other Chinese migrants who set up businesses in British territory, they normally benefitted from government support, as can be seen in Hastings response to Atchew's request. A few days after Atchew's letter was written, the following government advertisement appeared:

Fort William 5th November 1781

Whereas it has been represented to the Hon'ble the Governor General and Council by Atchew, a native of China now under the protection of this government, that several ill-disposed persons have endeavoured to entice away the Chinese laborers in his employee who are under indentures to him for a term of years. Notice is hereby given that the board wishing to grant every encouragement to the Colony of Chinese under the direction of Atchew are determined to afford him every support and assistance in up detecting such Persons and bringing them to condign punishment for inveigling away his people or affording them shelter from him.

By order of the Hon'ble Governor General and Council

(Sd) J. P. Auriol, Secretary[22]

The Chinese in India were recognised as hard-working and industrious; however, they suffered the same foibles as other people, as a police memo from 1788 suggests:

A number of Chinese have settled in Calcutta, who, tho' in general Sober and industrious, yet when intoxicated commit violent outrages, particularly against each other and as thro the difficulty procuring an interpreter it is almost impossible to ascertain who are the delinquents.[23]

Ellen Oxfeld studied Chinese migrants who arrived in India in the twentieth century. Opportunities in the Indian business environment were not as plentiful as many other nations, but once again, Chinese merchants rose to dominate their industry. A key factor in their success was the Chinese work ethic, as one migrant explains: 'It took me twenty years, twenty years to build this tannery. I didn't do it overnight.'[24] However, not everyone succeeded. Some who attempted to run their own business ended up changing their occupations or leaving the tanning district. Some opened restaurants while others emigrated once more.

Those that did succeed used the same business models that brought success in China and South East Asia. Standing out was the role of social networks. They drew upon their connections to establish themselves, commonly going into business with family members or others who came from the same village in China. They commonly worked in the family tannery, gaining knowledge and experience before branching out on their own. As one tannery owner states, 'Just as a tree sprouts many branches when it grows large, so too, when sons grow up they will establish separate households.'[25]

The businesses were family businesses, and the employment of non-family managers only occurred in the largest tanneries where there were insufficient family members to fill all the roles. However, the owners knew that these jobs were often used as stepping stones on the way to starting their own business after they have gained sufficient skills. As one said, 'you can never keep a good manager for long'[26].

This study revealed some of the more problematic sides of Chinese family businesses. The Chinese suffer the same impulses as other people, and there is always the possibility that someone will place self-interest above family hierarchy and solidarity. Competition between brothers is very common and a highly contentious period occurs on division of family property after either the death or retirement of the father. There is a need for agreement on division of funds, machinery and factory space if they are living in the tannery. If the brothers cannot agree between themselves, someone from their wider network, either the Industry Association or family surname group, will be brought in to adjudicate.

FAMILY FIRMS AND ETHNIC NETWORKS

Studies of businesses in the Philippines have found similar problems with Chinese family businesses. The father is the central authority around which everything hinges. Control is strongly personalised and centralised around him[27]. When he dies or chooses to relinquish control, conflicts among the children surface and this often leads to the business disintegrating. This problem is particularly acute when the business has grown so large that it no longer relies on the nuclear family, in which case children and grandchildren may fight to gain control of the business.

It is not surprising that many scholars believe in a 'three generation' theory of family businesses in which an entrepreneurial patriarch starts a business, which continues down to the next generation, but falls apart with the third generation[28]. Not only does the family structure undermine longevity, it also places limits on growth. Business growth requires additional resources, including managerial resources, which may go beyond that which the family can provide[29].

Nevertheless, when Chinese have successfully expanded, they have done it while retaining the family structure. For example, in the Philippines, when Chinese invested in downstream manufacturing, they often relied on subcontractors as opposed to vertical integration[30]. This enabled a business to expand its activities without having to employ outside managers. They simply contracted another family firm to do these activities for them.

When Chinese expand internationally, they also draw on traditional ethnic networks. The nature of the initial migration means that many ethnic Chinese have friends or relatives living in other countries. As one businessman said, 'wherever he went in South East Asia there was always someone there with whom he had some server connection and who was ready to help'[31]. He claimed this was a major factor in his success.

Businesses based in developing countries are very conscious of their technological, capital and managerial limitations. Consequently, when they invest offshore, they often prefer joint ventures with partners who have the resources that they lack. In this way, international expansion often occurs on a basis of joint ventures rather than complete ownership[32]. The offshore investment may exist as a company subsidiary, but equity is shared, and remains managed as a separate business, normally around the offshore Chinese family. There was little vertical integration as found in modern Western businesses.

During this expansion, even the largest regional conglomerates remained characterised by a family oriented structure. They remain in family control with patriarchal top management, while sons and daughters were typically given a division of the company to manage. When outside managers are used, they will be given managerial and technical roles, while family members retain the key custodial and entrepreneurial functions, thereby retaining control[33].

Although large conglomerates maintain their family focus, their resource base means they have options that smaller firms don't have. Large companies can expand internationally by full acquisition. Their large capital base enables them to pursue an expansion strategy of simply purchasing offshore companies. However, the companies they purchase commonly remain uncoordinated except at the financial level. These companies did not attain the more sophisticated integrative structures that existed in the West. The conglomerate grows to a huge size but its individual components remain small and highly diversified. It was in this way that the Salim group acquired hundreds of separate companies in many countries across a wide range of markets[34].

These family based structures might be efficient for small family firms, but they become inefficient as firms grow, and many companies have become aware of the need to adapt more efficient management structures. In recent decades, many traditional characteristics of Chinese business have been replaced by more modern approaches to business, particularly as the children have benefitted from Western-style business education. They have adopted structures more suited to the size and complexity of modern organisations. Top management may retain power, but decision making is increasingly decentralised, with more decisions delegated to lower-level managers.

They are also less likely to rely on clan groups or retained earnings for capital. The development of financial markets across Asia has aided this. Chinese businesses are more likely to refer to banks and financial institutions. They are also expanding outside their operations into new areas. Today, ethnic Chinese businesses in South East Asia are high performers in many industries. It has been the purpose of this chapter to explain how they got there.

CHAPTER 10

Evolution of the Art

....

THE ART OF CHINESE BUSINESS

The secrets of Chinese success begin in childhood. Chinese children are taught to work hard, value education and save rigorously. This can be seen in the merchant manuals which stressed the importance of teaching the value of money and hard work. To this day, the Chinese retain a reputation for hard work. The current generation of young Chinese may be less frugal than their ancestors, but the emphasis on hard work remains. Today, tiger mothers continue to force a strong work discipline upon their children, with the consequence that Chinese students gain higher grades in their studies than other ethnic groups.

Some authors have linked this work ethic and strong pursuit of wealth to a sense of insecurity[1]. As a people, they have experienced periods of extreme poverty and deprivation, and at other times the vagaries of control-obsessed governments. This encouraged the development of a strong work ethic and pursuit of wealth as a means of security[2]. Even when they migrated, the sense of being a besieged minority in countries dominated by other ethnic groups reinforced this belief that they must rely on their own resources.

The sense of frugality learned in childhood could be seen in a number of business practices that contributed to success. They strove to keep their expenses low. Chinese businessmen exercised rigorous control of their inventory. By keeping their stock levels low, it reduced the amount of capital they needed and also reduced the need for a loan and payment of interest. They also understood the importance of keeping a tight rein on cash flow[3]. This emphasis on cash flow could be seen in even the richest companies. For example, a board member of one of the largest Salim companies said:

> [Liem's] philosophy was the right one. He already knew what I learnt much later: You need to have a company with a continuous positive cash flow. With this you can borrow three times as much[4].

Some characteristics of Chinese business were only an advantage in specific environments. In China and South East Asia, businessmen were operating in environments characterised by high levels of uncertainty. Transportation and information technologies were very basic and this made it hard to get reliable market information. In this light, the business networks were the best available alternative for the management of information and seizing of opportunities.

Their networks compensated for market and information imperfections, and helped to distribute resources to where they were needed. In this way, they filled the gaps that existed where institutions were weak or, as one study described, they were 'fillers of potholes on the road to development'[5]. Within these networks, the relationships reduced transaction costs and enabled businessmen to identify opportunities and mobilise resources quickly, despite the limitations of the environment.

The 'Chinese trading company' was an ideal structure for such environments. Chinese businesses did not require a high level of investment in either capital or organisational structure. They had a loose structure which operated with great flexibility that enabled them to respond to opportunities wherever they arose. As deal makers, Chinese merchants could change their relationships and supply chains depending on what opportunity arose. In this way, they shared some characteristics with what today's organisational theorists call the 'network' structure. It is a flexible organisation based on informal relationships with other businesses that could be utilised as the need arises.

Again, the Salim group fits with this pattern despite its massive size. Anthony Salim, who took over as CEO of the group, noted the haphazard way in which the group evolved, saying, 'The group evolved not by design, but by necessity. Whatever opportunity was good, we just grabbed.'[6] The group seized every opportunity at hand, and consequently diversified in many different directions.

It wasn't just relationships with businessmen that were important. Forming alliances with political elites helped to remove political impediments to business. Political alliances could also provide market power, and Chinese merchants were very open to strategies that enhanced market dominance, including joint action with other businesses.

It has long been recognised that relationships in China were a substitute for what the law provided in the West[7]. In societies where the law cannot be relied upon to enforce business agreements, another mechanism is needed. Hence, Chinese businessmen cultivated *guanxi* (connections). A leading scholar on Chinese business, Gordon Redding, goes as far as saying that without these connections, 'nothing can be made to happen in China'.

These relationships provided advantages, but also obligations. If a businessman loses his reputation for trust, he will be severely handicapped in future business activities. Consequently, such relationships are driven by a strong set of ethical values and interpersonal obligations designed to create a sense of reliability. Maintaining 'face' was an important strategic consideration. However, this trust would only extend to those people that a businessman had developed a relationship with.

Working within a network was made easier by the common ethnic backgrounds, values and reputational effects. Many of these are based on Confucian values. The philosopher Confucius was once asked, 'Is there one word which may serve as a rule of practice for all one's life?' He answered, 'Is not reciprocity such a word? What you do not want done to yourself, do not do to others.'[8]

Chinese relationships were based on the principle of reciprocity[9]. Businessmen would operate with an 'implicit balance sheet of favors'[10], knowing that any favour done in the past would need to be repaid in the future. The result was a network in which businesses regularly supported one another. Through the exchange of favours, trust was built and maintained, and through this process, business-men gained assistance to achieve their business goals. And, of course, such relationships had the added advantage in that they could lead to deep friendships.

Other Confucian values could be seen in the practices of busi-ness networks and guilds. This included the offshore Chinese. For example, the Voluntary Associations in Singapore practised chari-table works and mutual assistance in a similar manner to those in China[11]. When businessmen operate with a common set of rules and values, it makes it easier to perform transactions with trust and understanding, and reduces the chance that opportunistic and exploitive behaviour occurs.

Of course, Confucianism could also be a huge impediment to business, particularly with the low ranking given to business and the consequent restrictions that businessmen regularly faced. Chinese migrants often did better in foreign countries than they did at home. When Chinese merchants ventured offshore and entered territories ruled by the Dutch and English, they enjoyed a more stable political environment. Here they encountered transparent rules and regula-tions, and the officials tasked with enforcing them did not stray from the law. Most important, these laws encouraged and protected trade[12].

At the heart of Confucian society was the family, and the family firm was the heart of Chinese business. Family firms were not unique to China and could be found in other countries; however, the family's position in state doctrine was unique to China. The value of any action could be judged by whether or not it contributed to the well-being of the family. Each person was committed to the welfare of their family, so kinship bonds were consistent with commercial loyalty. The father ran his business as a centralised decision maker confident in the loyalty of his children. With long-term security, the father could build significant knowledge of a market, and invest in relationships strengthened over time[13].

As an autocratic leader, the father was not encumbered with bureaucratic or procedural requirements. He could make a decision and commit resources quickly, knowing that his family would implement his will. And if he needed to draw on external resources, his long-established relationships would help him act with speed and minimal formalities.

Some characteristics of Chinese business could be a disadvantage to growth. The family firm meant that resources such as staff were limited by the size of the family. This could limit the potential for growth. Similarly, the tendency to undervalue services, such as research and development and legal advice, placed limits on the scope of their activities. Consequently, as they entered new markets and China itself modernised, Chinese businesses have had to change. In the following sections, we will describe how this pressure to change has been growing since the mid-nineteenth century.

THE SPARK FOR TRANSFORMATION: THE OPIUM WARS

In chapter eight, we described how the British began exporting opium to China in order to pay for their imports of tea and silk. The Chinese government would periodically embark on campaigns to stamp out the trade, but local officials were not committed to these campaigns. The opium trade had been a valuable source of income for officials, and it was reported that on seizing a drug boat, officials would continue to carry the drug themselves. In fact, since 1794, the sale had been standardised. Officials would let the opium cargo pass through on payment of a 'small gratuity'. Once these bribes were paid, the ships could comfortably move upriver to a quiet place where the stock was unloaded. There would be an occasional drive to clean up the trade, but these were generally perceived as opportunities for officials to squeeze local merchants for money[14].

In the 1830s, the opium trade soared. The 'annual average of the years 1835–9 was almost double that of the previous seven years'[15]. This led the government to impose another clampdown. As an indication of how the drug was perceived at the time, the campaign was believed to be driven more by a desire to stop the outflow of gold and silver, rather than an attempt to outlaw the drug.

As on previous occasions, local officials were not fully committed to the clampdown. Such was the level of Chinese collusion in the trade that the Court could not rely on them to bring the trade to an end. It was only with the appointment of an outsider with the intelligence and integrity of Commissioner Lin Tse-Hsu that serious efforts were made to bring the trade to an end. In 1839, he wrote to Queen Victoria requesting that she act 'in accordance with decent feeling' and support his efforts to suppress the trade. Commissioner Lin wrote:

> We find that your country is sixty or seventy thousand *li* from China. Yet there are barbarian ships that strive to come here for trade for the purpose of making a great profit. The wealth of China is used to profit the barbarians. That is to say, the great profit made by barbarians is all taken from the rightful share of China. By what right do they then in return use the poisonous drug to injure the Chinese people? Even though the barbarians may not necessarily intend to do us harm, yet

in coveting profit to an extreme, they have no regard for injuring others. Let us ask, where is your conscience?[16]

To deliver this letter, Lin Tse-Hsu was reliant on the traders sailing between Britain and China, but these were the very people whose actions he was trying to suppress. Unsurprisingly, the letter's delivery was delayed and by the time it arrived, actions had escalated to the point of war.

The Opium War delivered China a decisive defeat. Britain was not the first nation to defeat the Chinese, but unlike their predecessors, the Mongols and Manchurians, Britain had no intention of occupying China. They merely wanted to trade and it was to this end that the Treaty of Nanking was signed at the end of the war. The Treaty opened up five treaty ports along China's coast for trade. Foreign traders were no longer restricted to Canton, thereby bringing an end to the Co-Hong's monopoly. At the treaty ports, foreign merchants were free to trade with whoever they wished. Britain also gained the right to send consuls to the ports and communicate directly with Chinese officials. The Treaty also established a system of fixed tariffs which reduced the chance of fleecing by the mandarins.

The Treaty of Nanking also ceded Hong Kong island to the British but, at the time, this was not seen as much of a prize. The British foreign secretary, Lord Palmerston, described it as 'a barren island with hardly a house upon it'[17]. However, Hong Kong thrived under the British who built the island into an important centre of trade. Chinese immigrants flooded into the British territory which became a haven when civil strife wracked the mainland. On arrival, they found a government that recognised the importance of business. In Hong Kong, Chinese merchants were free from interference by the mandarins. The British kept it simple, and respected the Chinese work ethic and ability to turn a profit. In this environment, the Chinese thrived.

Hong Kong developed into a major entrepôt, a mid-link between China and South East Asia. As Chinese emigrated to other parts of the world, including the United States, it created an international market for Chinese goods. The Chinese moving to places like San Francisco wanted to buy the Chinese products they had grown up consuming, and it was through Hong Kong that many of these goods flowed[18].

Other Western nations quickly followed Britain in signing 'unequal treaties' with China, and gained extra-terrestrial rights at the treaty ports. The most important of the treaty ports was Shanghai which, by 1870, accounted for two thirds of China's foreign trade. By 1931, it was the recipient of almost half of the direct foreign invest-ment flowing into China[19].

There is a myth that Shanghai was a little village until the British came along, but this is not true. While there is no doubt that the port boomed under the treaty system, it was by no means a village before-hand. Shanghai had served as a coastal port as early as the Song and Yuan dynasties[20]. It declined during the early Ming dynasty's economic contraction, but recovered as the dynasty progressed and market forces were re-established. By 1730, an imperial edict recog-nised Shanghai as a leading port when the region's river and sea customs office was relocated there. By 1735, it was the major port of entry and exit for coastal traffic of the lower Yangtze, including the prosperous Jiangnan region. By 1832–4, it was recognised as one of the leading ports in the world, ten years before the British victory.

Foreign encroachment into China did not stop at the ports. Over the following years, conflicts were used by foreign nations to extract more concessions. To the Chinese, this encroachment came to be known as the 'carving of the Chinese melon', a deeply felt humili-ation. Each defeat caused the Chinese people to question the legitimacy of their weak and ineffective government. This led to a period of great instability with domestic uprisings and civil war. The worst of these was the Taiping rebellion which lasted from 1850 to 1864 and cost more than twenty million lives, the most deadly conflict in the world during the nineteenth century.

THE SCIENCE OF BUSINESS AND WAR

How did the once mighty China become so weak? Until the Opium Wars, China was confident of its superiority and treated foreigners as uncultured barbarians. Britain forced the Chinese to face reality. Britain was a small country with a population of about 18.5 million[21]. By contrast, China was a giant of approximately 410 million. What made the Chinese decline more pronounced was the fact that Britain was on the other side of the world. It could only send a portion of its military power, yet it demolished Chinese forces on sea and land.

Militarily, China lost because the Europeans drew on new technologies. For example, the British warship *Nemesis* was powered by a steam engine which completely outmanoeuvred the wind-powered sails of their enemy. Similarly, the superior British weaponry destroyed the junks in the Chinese navy. Technology also made a difference on land, as the British rifles could fire faster and more accurately than the matchlock muskets and artillery they faced.

This influence of technology also reflected the changing balance in business practices. Western companies were applying advances in knowledge to all aspects of business. These knowledge gains spanned the full range of productive activities from mechanical engineering to chemistry, mining to production – Westerners drew on science to create new products and processes that China's science base could not deliver.

As the nineteenth century progressed, Chinese business fell further and further behind. In the West, the development of electricity gave birth to completely new industries for domestic and industrial consumers. Even the oldest industries, such as agriculture, experienced scientific revolution as advanced knowledge of biology, ecology and chemistry led to more effective land use and animal management techniques.

Some of the biggest advances came when science was applied to management. Jobs and industrial processes were analysed in a systematic way, with the intention of finding the best use of labour. The result was 'scientific management' which was applied to one industry after another and helped propel the United States to economic leadership at the end of the nineteenth century. In the twentieth century, the new science of psychology would also lead to improvements in human resource management, as well as more effective marketing.

It could be said that while the Chinese were masters of the 'art' of business, Westerners were developing the 'science' of business. In the first chapter, we defined business as the art of value provision. Westerners were now practising the science of value provision. By science, we mean the systemised collection and understanding of knowledge. In the West, this knowledge was increasingly used in business. Not that the old techniques disappeared, and today, it is probably more accurate to say that business is both a science and an art.

CHINA IN THE TWENTIETH CENTURY

In 1911, the Qing dynasty was finally overthrown, bringing an end to two thousand years of imperial rule. On 1 January 1912, a republic was announced, but this did not herald a period of peace and progression. Differing political views combined with regional self-interest to create an ongoing period of civil war.

Chiang Kai-shek, the military leader for the Nationalist Unity Part (Kuomintang) succeeded in unifying the country in 1927 with the help of the Communists led by Mao Tse Tung. However, three weeks after their combined forces defeated their enemies, Chiang Kai-shek turned on his allies, executing thousands of them. After a series of attacks, the weakened Communists endured the now cele-brated 'long March': a six thousand mile retreat to Yan'an in Shaanxi province. This remote part of northern China remained their base until after World War II, while Chiang Kai Shek consolidated his control of the nation.

However, the general was about to experience his own problems. In 1931, Japan invaded Manchuria turning the northern Chinese province into a Japanese colony. Six years later, Japan attacked the rest of China in a precursor to World War II. One might think that Chiang Kai Shek's government would provide a useful ally to the United States in their fight against the Japanese, and the Americans certainly sought his co-operation. But Chiang Kai Shek had his own ambitions and was more interested in using his troops to blockade the communists in the north.

In the meantime, the Communists realised that if they were to succeed, they had to get popular support, so maintained a strict code of conduct when dealing with the local population. Unlike other warlords that abused peasants and stole their grain, the Communists grew much of their own food and paid for the food they acquired from others. They even helped peasants with their farm work. As a consequence, the Communist army grew in prestige, with a reputa-tion for self-reliance and a co-operative spirit. Consequently, when World War II ended and the civil war broke out again, it was the Communists who had the greatest support.

By October 1949, the Communists had enough support to defeat the Nationalists and establish the People's Republic of China. Chiang Kai Shek fled to Taiwan with a large number of his supporters. This brought to Taiwan a huge influx of capital and entrepreneurial talent that would help boost that island's economy. Hong Kong, still under

British rule, received a similar influx of talent and capital from the mainland.

China was now firmly in the hands of the Communists, driven by the ideology of Marx and Lenin but, in many ways, the new economy shared characteristics with that which had existed prior to the Tang dynasty and again in the early Ming dynasty. It was characterised by central government decision making, an emphasis on equality and restrictions on free enterprise.

The conflict between social equality and economic growth is one that all societies must contend with, but China has struggled with it more than most. A key strength of the market economy is that it provides incentives for hard work and economic growth. It also provides effective decentralised decision making rather than central-ised control by government. However, it also results in disparities in income and power, and the close relationships that merchants build with government officials has often resulted in corruption.

The Communists in China sought to avoid the weaknesses of the free market. They wanted a more equal society, yet social disparities still appeared under Communism. Chairman Mao felt that a new elite was forming, comprised of high government officials, adminis-trators and educated people. These people had a power and income denied to the ordinary person[22]. Mao responded by appealing to the common people to support change. He instigated the Cultural Revolution in which younger people were encouraged to challenge power holders. Bureaucrats were attacked and universities were closed. An emphasis was placed on holding the correct ideology. People with the wrong ideas were victimised, with the effect that people became afraid to speak out or make decisions. The conse-quence was society became even more hierarchal and centralised.

A major component of the Cultural Revolution was the attack on 'capitalist roaders', that is, people whose ideas could lead to the restoration of capitalism. One of those accused was Deng Xiaoping.

He was attacked for trying to prevent the ill-treatment of other leaders and 'playing bridge with people whose relatives had been capitalists'. Members of the Red Guard threw Deng's son from a four-storey building, paralysing him. Deng himself may have been saved from worse treatment because of his friendship with Mao, but he was still paraded around Beijing wearing a dunce's cap[23]. However, Deng Xiaoping was no dunce. In the years to come, he would establish China's third commercial revolution and, in so doing, raise the nation to a new level of prosperity.

BUSINESS MAKES CHINA GREAT AGAIN

In 1976, Chairman Mao died and Deng Xiaoping emerged as China's most powerful man. Deng Xiaoping was a pragmatist and recognised that the solution must fit the problem. His most famous maxim is, 'It doesn't matter whether a cat is white or black, as long as it catches mice.' Although a confirmed socialist, he was not restricted by ideology. He was aware that socialism was superior to capitalism in dealing with issues of equity, but his attitude became more sophisticated over time. He accepted that equity did not necessarily mean equality. However, he was concerned with the polarisation that occurs when large gaps exist between the rich and poor. A society should deliver common prosperity and eliminate poverty[24].

Equity is not attained when people are equally experiencing poverty, but that was the situation Deng inherited when he took control. China's GDP per capita was a mere US$100 per year. Hence he recognised the need for change and instituted the reforms that have created the current phenomenal growth in China. Although he was the architect of these reforms, he did not begin with a clear objective. His reforms unfolded in a gradual, evolutionary fashion[25].

One of his first reforms occurred in agriculture. Under the old system, the country's farms had been grouped together to form collective farms. However, communal ownership removed the incentive for individuals to work hard. They got no personal reward for any extra work they provided, a situation made worse by government intervention dictating what they produced. Recognising that Sichuan was one of the poorest regions in the country, Deng gave its farmers the freedom to experiment. The locals made the decision to de-collectivise and allow more private ownership. Farmers gained more control over what they produced and output soared.

Although Deng approved all major policies, he was aware of the benefits of delegation. He was a hands-off leader who set the general policy direction but left the detail to others[26]. He personally noted that his success in reforming agriculture came from delegating decisions to the locals, saying, 'The main idea is to delegate power to lower levels. The main reason our rural reform has been so successful is that we gave peasants the power to make decisions and that stimulated their initiative.'[27]

This is a huge change in government management from that which existed under the Communists. No longer was central government telling people how to do things. One commentator stated that Deng Xiaoping mastered the art of laissez-faire, the ruler's art of non-acting[28]. This description is a clear link to Taoism. A famous chapter of the *Tao Te Ching* describes the best leaders, saying:

> The best leaders value their words, and use them sparingly.
>   When they have accomplished their task,
>   the people say, 'Amazing!
>   We did it, all by ourselves!'[29]

With greater freedom, farmers and other small businesses began producing for consumer demand, not what the state decreed. After decades of socialism, China had re-discovered its business heritage[30]. This was the beginning of China's third great commercial revolution and the period of prosperity that we are still seeing today.

However, freedom and decentralisation would not be sufficient by themselves to raise prosperity to Western standards. The country's business techniques had slipped well behind the rest of the world, and in a 1978 speech, Deng stressed the need to build its base on science and technology[31]. The following year, the government launched a policy of modernisation in agriculture, industry, science and technology, and defence.

Aware of the importance of foreign capital and technology, an Open Door Policy was introduced in 1979 which welcomed foreign investment into the country[32]. This process of opening was done gradually, beginning with the establishment of four 'Special Economic Zones' (SEZ) in coastal areas where foreigners were allowed to form joint ventures in specific sectors[33]. This process enabled the Chinese to gain capital and knowledge of modern production techniques. As the benefits of the policy became apparent, the policy was expanded and now every region is eligible for foreign direct investment.

Initially foreign companies were slow to invest in China. Memories of the recent Cultural Revolution led foreigners to take a 'wait and see' approach until they could be confident in the new government. Nevertheless, between 1979 and 1983, the value of foreign direct investment (FDI) increased from $0.5 billion to $1.5 billion[34]. With more liberalisation in policy, the years between 1984 and 1991 saw a rapid increase in capital inflows and, by 1992, China was the second largest recipient of FDI in the world[35]. Through this process, China was able to develop its industrial base, introduce new technologies, and upgrade managerial and labour skills.

Initially, most of the foreign capital came from overseas Chinese. In 1987, 70 per cent of FDI came from Macao, Taiwan, Malaysia, Singapore and Hong Kong which, at this stage, was still in the hands of the British[36]. Ethnic and cultural affinity raised understanding and confidence to invest. There was also the advantage of geographic proximity, especially for Macao and Hong Kong. Overseas Chinese investors also included Indonesia's Salim group who we discussed in the last chapter.

By 2005, it was estimated that more than 100,000 joint ventures had been established by overseas Chinese, mainly in Guangdong and Fujian provinces[37]. An example is the Charoen Pokphand (CP) Group, a company established in Thailand by two brothers who migrated there in 1919 from Guangdong. The brother's early business specialised in farm-seed, before expanding to other related product lines including animal feeds, chicken farming and processing. In 1981, they set up their first venture in China, Conti Chia Tai, in Shenzhen. Over time it expanded so that, by 2005, it boasted operations in twenty-six of China's thirty provinces[38].

In some cases, offshore governments became investors. The Chinese premier Deng Xiaoping, had been impressed with Singapore's economic transformation since it gained independence from Britain so he invited Singapore's prime minister Lee Kuan Yew to develop a model industrial township within China. The result of this inter-governmental agreement was the China-Singapore Suzhou Industrial Park[39].

In the 1990s, non-Chinese sources of investment became more important. In 1994, the United States became the third largest source, while Japan was recorded as the second largest in 1995[40]. However, the overseas Chinese as a group still constituted 54 per cent as late as 1997[41].

Hong Kong businesses were particularly active investors just across the border in Shenzhen. A number of factors motivated the investors. First, Hong Kong businesses were very aware of the cheap labour advantages in relocating factories to China. They also noted that, as China got richer, it provided a growing market for their goods. There was also talk that the British would relinquish control of Hong Kong island and return it to China, an event that eventually happened in 1997. The extent of Chinese investment can be seen in the textile and clothing industries. In 1995, 96 per cent of Shenzhen's textile industry and 95 per cent of its garments industry were owned by investors from Hong Kong[42]. Soon, most Hong Kong companies had relocated their production across the border in the Shenzhen and Guangzhou regions.

Shenzhen is perhaps the best symbol of the Chinese growth. In 1979, when it was established as one of the first four Special Economic Zones, its population was around 300,000. It possessed no industrial base, and its only advantage was its proximity to Hong Kong. Twenty years later, its population had grown to four million and, today, is in the vicinity of twelve million. The growth in output is even more impressive. In the 1980s and 1990s, China registered impressive GDP growth rates of 8 to 8.5 per cent per annum. At the same time, the real GDP of the Shenzhen SEZ grew at an annual average of 28.5 per cent, making it an important driver of China's commercial transformation[43].

Chinese industry grew on the basis of foreign investment, state intervention and a massive mobilisation of capital and cheap labour. Initially, growth was export led, but with the rise in China's wealth, domestic consumption is increasingly driving growth[44].

THE CHANGING ART OF BUSINESS

If firms were going to reap the full benefits of China's new market economy, they would have to modernise their business practices and structures. In many cases these changes were forced upon them by their own success. As their firms grew bigger, the founding patriarchs became overwhelmed with information and had no choice but to delegate decision making to professional managers who were not kin nor friends. Their businesses grew so big that they simply did not have sufficient numbers of relatives who had the expertise to fill these roles.

Changes in business practice have been facilitated by the increased number of Chinese acquiring Western-style business education. Many Chinese have gone offshore to gain an MBA or undergraduate business degree, and universities within China are increasingly adopting Western education methods. At the same time, many young Chinese are gaining exposure to foreign work practices when working in joint ventures or subsidiaries of multinational companies.

Peter Woo of Hong Kong's Wharf Group reflects the new breed of Chinese business person. Woo holds an MBA from Columbia University and had early work experience in Chase Manhattan Bank. As early as 1992, he signalled the changing practices, saying there 'are no friends in finance. The world has changed. They [old-style Chinese entrepreneurs] need to realize we are in a world market and need an international culture.'[45]

In an age of globalisation, Chinese firms are required to follow international accounting standards and business norms characterised by credible and transparent financial practices and management control. When Chinese firms enter new markets, they must adhere to the rules and regulations of the nations they are entering. To raise finance, they became less reliant on ethnic networks and made greater use of international financial markets to secure access to capital in order to fund their internationalisation efforts[46].

Changes in business practice have also been occurring in ethnic Chinese firms in other parts of Asia. The old paternalistic structure based on personal relationships and ethnic networks is increasingly being replaced by decentralisation and transparent financial performance[47]. Ethnic Chinese businesses throughout South East Asia have experienced management and organisational transformations, becoming more professional along the Western model. Senior members have seen their power declining and there has been a rise in the status of females[48].

In Indonesia, Anthony Salim represents this new breed. Educated in the United Kingdom, he is fully aware of the need to change from the business practices his grandfather used, saying, 'We have to transform ourselves to manage our resources; to transform our assets . . . We believe we operate in different markets.'[49]

A number of factors have helped to accelerate these changes. First was the Asian economic crisis of the 1990s which led to a raft of institutional reforms throughout East Asia. More transparency was sought in the political process, and this led to an end to monopolies and the collapse of political-economic alliances[50]. In some cases, these changes were forced upon governments by the International Monetary Fund (IMF) who wanted greater transparency and less corruption. This meant that the old strategies of maximising market power through political relationships were no longer available. The financial and large corporate sectors were particularly targeted[51].

The second factor accelerating change in business practice is globalisation, which has made the business environment more competitive. Globalisation is changing the rules of the game in Asia and has led to a revision of competitive rules and related institutions. Businesses can no longer hide behind monopolistic protection given to them by political cronies. They must develop 'competitive advantages based on organisational competence rather than on monopolistic licences or political favours'[52].

However, it would be wrong to say that the old style of Chinese capitalism has been completely replaced by Western models. Henry Yeung[53] of the National University of Singapore noticed that despite these changes some elements of continuity exist. The family firm remains a central unit of Chinese business. Transformation of business both in and outside China is not a linear process. Business practice oscillates between the old and the new[54]. They had to modernise to accommodate growth, but opportunities will often appear that are too good to refuse and these will be seized using the old deal-making characteristics.

Yeung believes a hybrid business model is emerging[55]. A transformation process is occurring in which some distinctive elements of ethnic Chinese capitalism are being morphed and recombined with modern elements. The result is something that is 'neither ethnic Chinese capitalism as we knew it nor global capitalism', but a hybrid form of ethnic Chinese capitalism. Nevertheless, he notes that 'as ethnic Chinese capitalism is increasingly engaging with globalizing forces, its core features will be changed and reshaped.'

Business Not War!

Those who swagger will eat bitterness. This is the way of the world.

Song of caution in the *Shanggu xingmi*

The contemporary world is an exciting place for China and its trade partners who, by practising the art and science of business, are enjoying a reciprocated economic growth. However, some historical problems remain. The age-old problem associated with markets is the growing inequalities between rich and poor, and this problem is re-emerging.

China has always struggled with variations in status and wealth, but these problems have not been limited to internal relations. Historically, China's elite always looked down upon foreigners. This could be seen as far back as the Opium Wars. In fact, some people consider this to be the main cause of the war. While there is no doubt that the basis of the war was the opium trade, another contributor was the way the Chinese government treated foreigners. Businessmen like Howqua may have treated foreigners as friends and equals, but government officers looked upon them as inferior barbarians. The importance of this was noted by nations that were neutral during the war. For example, the United States president John Quincy Adams identified this as a principle cause of the conflict. He stated that opium was:

> . . . a mere incident to the dispute . . . the cause of the war is the kowtow—the arrogant and insupportable pretensions of China that she will hold commercial intercourse with the rest of mankind not upon terms of equal reciprocity, but upon the insulting and degrading forms of the relations between lord and vassal[56].

The merchant manual *Shanggu xingmi* warns businessmen to avoid having too great a sense of oneself saying, 'Those who swagger will eat bitterness. This is the way of the world.' Sadly, this advice was directed at businessmen and was not heeded by government officials. China's century of humiliation was preceded by a century of arrogance and bullying, and it was inevitable that at some point it would get a bloody nose. Sadly, the Chinese people suffered as a consequence of their leaders' arrogance.

China was, and still is, a status-based society. Jun Wang from Jinan University contrasts this with 'good points of the Western culture' which advocates 'individualism and law spirits'[57]. Western culture is strongly influenced by Christianity in which every individual has a soul, and is equal in the eyes of God. By contrast, in China 'the people thought it ridiculous that all were equal before the law'.

A Confucian society is status-based with some people given more importance than others. Yet, those Chinese who have emigrated to other parts of the world illustrated through their success that they were not inferior to their masters. When given the opportunity, they could soar. Nevertheless, many in China have recognised the folly of this outlook, including Chairman Mao, who introduced the Cultural Revolution partly to remove the elitist elements from Chinese society.

Chinese business has regularly suffered from this outlook, and it is no surprise that many academics have argued that Confucianism has hindered the development of commerce. One can't help but wonder if the Legalist belief, that everyone was equal before the law, was maintained, more respect would have been given to the individual. In as much as China is currently rediscovering its business heritage, it may be that it needs to rediscover another part of its heritage: the Legalist desire for greater equality (but without the harsh extremes of Legalism).

Modern analyses of Chinese business still identify the strong influence of status. China is described as a high 'power distance' culture in which there are substantial gaps between those at the top of an organisation and those on the bottom rung. However, some of these gaps may disappear over time as China modernises its business practices. There are significant advantages to a business which practices decentralised decision making with power and authority delegated to lower levels. Such changes also raise the self-esteem and sense of worth in those working at the lower levels. It is perhaps ironic that Chairman's Mao's quest for a more equal society may in time be achieved through capitalism.

However, the biggest danger to Chinese prosperity may not come from those that practise the art of business, but from those that practise the art of war. As the Chinese economy has grown, the government has more funds available to finance its military and, as this book goes to press, the Chinese military has been building new bases in the South China Sea that could threaten the

Philippines and Japan. If this does escalate to the point where war breaks out, it will reduce welfare for all concerned, including China. It is a sad fact that relationships built by businessmen to enhance prosperity can be quickly destroyed by military action.

To those of us whose lives have been enriched by Chinese trade and friendships, we can only hope that wise heads prevail. Through the art and science of business, we exchange goods and build relationships that make our lives richer. In enabling this process, governments can enhance the welfare and prosperity of all.

Notes

....

CHAPTER 1: THE ART OF BUSINESS

1. Ibn Battuta (1994) *The Travels of Ibn Battuta AD 1325–1354* (translated by Defremery, C., and Sanguinettu, B. R., ed. by Gibb, H. A. R.). London: The Hakluyt Society, p.814.

2. Sun Tzu (2004) *The Art of War* (translated by Giles, L., Project Gutenberg). Downloaded from http://www.gutenberg.org/cache/epub/132/pg132-images.html

3. Verse 17 of the *Tao Te Ching*. Lao Tzu (2000) *Tao Te Ching* (translated by Hinton, D.). Washington DC: Counterpoint.

4. Wilhelm, R. and Baynes, C. F. (translators) (1961) *The I Ching or Book of Changes*. New York: Bollingen Pantheon, p.129.

5. Chang, Y. N. (1976) 'Early Chinese Management Thought.' *California Management Review*, 19(2), 71–76.

6. Kat Tai Tam (2009) *The Social Status and Thought of Merchants in Ming China, 1368–1644: A Foray the Social Effects of the Commercialization of Ming China*. Downloaded from http://qspace.library.queensu.ca/jspui/bitstream/1974/5149/1/Tam_Kat_Tai_200908_MA.pdf

7. Knoblock, J. and Riegel, J. (2000) *The Annals of Lü Buwei: A Complete Translation and Study*. Stanford: Stanford University Press, p.4.

8. Knoblock and Riegel (2000) p.4.

9. All excerpts from Ames, R. T. and Rosemont Jr, H. (1998) *The Analects of Confucius: A Philosophical Translation*. New York: Ballantine Books.

10. Kat Tai Tam (2009) p.8.

11. Ibid.

12. Brook, T., (2004) *Confusions of Pleasure: Commerce and Culture in Ming China*. University of California Press, p.69.

CHAPTER 2: THE TANG AND SONG COMMERCIAL REVOLUTION

1. Tao Ch'ien (northern Song) Collected poems by the Ts'an-liao Master, cited in Yoshinobu, S. (1992) *Commerce and Society in Sung China* (translated by Elvin, M.) Michigan abstracts of Chinese and Japanese works on Chinese History, No.2, University of Michigan, p.154.
2. Liu, W. G. (2015) *The Chinese Market Economy 1000–1500*. Albany: State University of New York Press.
3. Ibid., p.84.
4. Li Ch'ao (early ninth century) cited in Yoshinobu (1992) p.5.
5. Liu (2015) p.90.
6. Yeh Shih (twelfth century) cited in Yoshinobu (1992) p.14.
7. Liu (2015) p.87.
8. Twitchett, D. (1966) 'The Tang Market System', *Asia Major*, 12(2) 202–48.
9. Yoshinobu (1992).
10. Liu (2015) p.69.
11. Chou Mi, Ts'ao-ch'uang yun-yu, cited in Yoshinobu (1992) p.145.
12. Liu (2015) p.20.
13. Yoshinobu (1992).
14. Twitchett (1966).
15. Ibid., p.243.
16. Ibid., p.244.
17. Ibid., p.247.
18. Ibid., p.245.
19. Ibid.
20. Ibid., pp.229–30.
21. Liu (2015).
22. Wu Yung cited in Yoshinobu (1992) p.52.
23. Liu (2015).
24. Ibid.
25. Yeh Shao-Weng cited in Yoshinobu (1992) p.46.
26. Hartwell, R. (1967) 'A cycle of economic change in imperial China: coal and iron in northeast China, 750–1350.' *Journal of the Economic and Social History of the Orient*, 10(1), 102–59.
27. Ibid.

28. Ibid.

29. Hartwell, R. (1966) 'Markets, technology, and the structure of enterprise in the development of the eleventh-century Chinese iron and steel industry.' *The Journal of Economic History*, 26(01), 29–58.

30. Liu (2015) p.91.

31. Hsu Meng-hsin (1137) San-ch'ao pei-meng hui pien, cited in Yoshinobu (1992) p.32.

32. Hartwell (1966) p.32.

33. Ibid., p.43.

34. Hartwell (1967).

35. Hartwell (1966), p.35.

36. Eberhard, W. (1957) 'Wang Ko, An Early Industrialist.' *Oriens*, 248–52.

CHAPTER 3: HOW DID MERCHANTS MAKE MONEY? – THE TIME-SPACE DIMENSION

1. Ts'ai Hsiang cited in Yoshinobu, S. (1992) *Commerce and Society in Sung China* (translated by Elvin, M.) Michigan abstracts of Chinese and Japanese works on Chinese History, No.2, University of Michigan, p.185.

2. Yoshinobu (1992) p.74.

3. Ibid.

4. Extract from *Solutions for Merchants* cited in Lufrano, R. J. (1997) *Honorable Merchants: Commerce and Self Cultivation in Late Imperial China*. University of Hawaii Press, p.142.

5. Zhang Han cited in Brook, T. (1981) 'The Merchant Network in 16th Century China: A Discussion and Translation of Zhang Han's "On Merchants".' *Journal of the Economic and Social History of the Orient/ Journal de l'histoire economique et sociale de l'Orient*, pp.165–214.

6. Lufrano (1997) p.136.

7. Ibid., p.134.

8. Yoshinobu (1992) p.59.

9. Polo, M. (1958) *The Travels* (translated by Latham, R. E.). London: Penguin, p.159

10. Lufrano (1997) p.10.

11. Ibid p.81.

12. Extract from *Essentials for Gentry and Merchants* cited in Andrews, M. (2011) *Cultures of Commerce Compared: A Comparative Study of the Ideal of the Businessman in China and England, c. 1600-1800* (Doctoral dissertation, London School of Economics).

13. Extract from *Essential Business* cited in Lufrano (1997) p.133.

14. Extract from *Encyclopedia for Gentry and Merchants* cited in Lufrano (1997) p.133.

15. Extract from *Essential Business* cited in Lufrano (1997) p.133.

16. Chu Hsi cited in Yoshinobu (1992) p.71.

17. Kung-k'eui cited in Yoshinobu (1992), p.73.

18. Chang Chung-tzu cited in Yoshinobu (1992) p.73.

19. Nait te weng (1235) *Splendours of the Capital* cited in Yoshinobu (1992) p.174.

20. Wu Tzu mu cited in Yoshinobu (1992) p.174.

21. Yoshinobu (1992) p.199.

22. *Essential Business* cited in Lufrano (1997) p.152.

23. Yoshinobu (1992) p.129.

24. Ibid, p.194.

25. Adapted from Yoshinobu (1992) p.79.

26. Extract from *Ming Encyclopedia of Matters of Everyday Use*, cited in Yoshinobu (1992) p.37.

27. Yoshinobu (1992).

28. Lufrano (1997).

29. Yoshinobu (1992) p.192.

30. Ibid., p.191.

31. Ibid., p.77.

32. Brook, T. (1998) *The Confusions of Pleasure: Commerce and culture in Ming China.* University of California Press, p.59.

33. Yoshinobu (1992) p.36.

34. Wang, J. (1999) *Entrepreneurship, Institutional Structures and Business Performance of the Overseas Chinese* (Discussion Paper No. 252).

35. From a twelfth-century letter written by Yang Wan-li to the famous statesman Yu Yun-wen cited in Yoshinobu (1992) p.29.

CHAPTER 4: INTERNATIONAL TRADE: SOUTHERN SONG TO EARLY MING

1. Whitfield, S. (2004) *The Silk Road: Trade, travel, war and faith*. Chicago: Serindia Publications.
2. Elisseeff, V. (2000) 'Approaches old and new to the silk roads', in *The Silk Roads: Highways to culture and commerce*, ed. by Elisseeff, V. Berghahn Books, pp.1–26.
3. Whitfield (2004).
4. Twitchett, D. (1966) 'The Tang Market System', *Asia Major*, 12(2): 202–48, p.233.
5. Ibid., p.224.
6. Ibid., p.224.
7. Shagdar, B. (2000) 'The Mongol Empire in the thirteenth and fourteenth centuries', in *The Silk Roads: Highways to culture and commerce*, ed. by Elisseeff, V. Berghahn Books, pp.127–44.
8. Finlay, R. (2010) *The Pilgrim Art: Cultures of porcelain in world history*. University of California Press, Berkeley and Los Angeles.
9. Polo Marco (1958) *The Travels of Marco Polo*. London: Penguin Books, p.113.
10. Ibid., p.130.
11. Ibid., p.210.
12. Ibid., p.209.
13. Twitchett (1966).
14. Wang Gungwu (1991) *China and the Chinese Overseas*. Singapore: Times Academic Press.
15. Lenz, W. (1997) 'Voyages of Admiral Zheng He Before Columbus', in Mathews, K. S. (ed.), *Shipbuilding and Navigation in the Indian Ocean Region AD 1400–1800*. New Delhi: Munshiram Manoharlal Publishers, p.147.
16. Dupoizat, M. F. (1995) 'The Ceramic Cargo of a Song Dyansty Junk Found in the Philippines and its Significance in the China-South East Asian Trade', in Scott, Rosemary and Guy, John (eds.), *South East Asia and China: Art, Interaction and Commerce*, pp.205–24, p.205.
17. Levathes, L. (1994) *When China Ruled the Seas: The treasure fleet of the Dragon Throne 1405–33*. New York: Simon & Schuster, p.43.
18. Yoshinobu (1970) p.7.

19. Chuimei, Ho, (1995) 'Intercultural Influence between China and South East Asia as Seen in Historical Ceramics', in Scott, R. and Guy, J. (eds), *South East Asia and China: Art Interaction and Commerce*, pp.118–40, p.118.

20. Beamish, J. (1995) 'The Significance of Yuan Blue and White Exported to South East Asia', in Scott, R. and Guy, J. (eds), *South East Asia and China: Art Interaction and Commerce*, pp.225–51, p.234.

21. Chang Hsieh (1618) cited in Yoshinobu (1970) p.16.

22. Yoshinobu (1970) p.40.

23. Hodder, R. (1996) *Merchant Princes of the East*. Chichester: Wiley.

24. Kay, J. (1995) *Why Firms Succeed: Choosing markets and challenging competitors to add value*. Oxford University Press, p.54.

25. Clark, H. R. (1991) *Community, Trade and Networks: Southern Fujian province from the third to the thirteenth century*. Cambridge University Press, p.134.

26. Liu (2015) p.3.

27. Polo (1958) p.237.

28. Yoshinobu (1970) p.28.

29. Su Tung-p'o cited in Yoshinobu (1970) p.187.

30. Gungwu (1991).

31. Ibid.

32. Ibid.

33. Ibid.

34. Polo (1958) p.237.

35. Ibn Battuta (1994) *The Travels of Ibn Battuta* AD 1325–1354 (translation by Defremery C., Sanguinettu, B. R., ed. by Gibb, H. A. R.). London: The Hakluyt Society, p.812.

36. Ibid., p.813.

37. Ibid., p.814.

38. Ibid., p.894

39. Clark (1991).

40. Ibn Battuta (1994) p.889.

41. Ibid., pp.893–4.

42. Ibid., pp.892–3.

43. Clark (1991).

44. Ibid. p.133.

45. Ibn Battuta (1994) p.900.

46. Gungwu (1991).

47. Ibid.

48. Lin, Lee Chor (1995) 'Textiles in Sino-South East Asian Trade: Song, Yuan and Ming dynasties', in Scott and Guy, *South East Asia and China: Art Interaction and Commerce*, pp.171–86, p.175.

49. Finlay (2010) p.215.

50. Yamauchi, Kiyoshi (1999) 'Comparison of Two Premodern Trade Manuals from England and China'. Downloaded from http://klibredb. lib.kanagawau.ac.jp/dspace/bitstream/10487/4070/1/kana-14-16-17-0019.pdf

51. Ibid., p.382.

52. Ibid., p.382.

53. Ibid., p.382.

CHAPTER 5: MING DYNASTY (1368–1644)

1. Brook, T. (1981) 'The Merchant Network in 16th Century China: A Discussion and Translation of Zhang Han's "On Merchants".' *Journal of the Economic and Social History of the Orient/Journal de l'histoire economique et sociale de l'Orient*, 165–214, p.186.

2. Dillon, M. (1989) 'The Merchants of Huizhou Commerce and Confucianism.' *History Today*, 39, 24–30.

3. Brook, T. (2004) *Confusions of Pleasure: Commerce and culture in Ming China*. University of California Press.

4. Liu (2015).

5. Ibid.

6. Ibid.

7. Brook (2004) p.48.

8. Ibid.

9. Dillon, M. (1976) *A history of the porcelain industry in Jingdezhen* (Doctoral dissertation, University of Leeds).

10. Ibid.

11. Dillon (1989).

12. Lufrano, R. J. (1997) *Honorable Merchants: Commerce and self-cultivation in late Imperial China*. University of Hawaii Press, p.47.

13. Gu Tanwu cited in Dillon (1989) pp.25–6.

14. Cited in Dillon, *History Today* p.28.
15. Dillon (1989).
16. Ibid.
17. Wang Taokun cited in Dillon (1989) pp.26–8.
18. Dillon, M. (1992) 'Transport and Marketing in the Development of the Jingdezhen Porcelain Industry during the Ming and Qing Dynasties.' *Journal of the Economic and Social History of the Orient/Journal de l'histoire economique et sociale de l'Orient*, 278–90.
19. Ibid.
20. Dillon (1989).
21. Ibid.
22. Brook (1981) p.173.
23. Ibid., p.190.
24. Ibid., p.168.
25. Ibid., p.208.
26. Ibid., p.208.
27. Ibid., p.197.
28. Brook (1981).
29. Ibid., p.205.
30. Ibid., p.205.
31. Ho, P. T. (1954) 'The salt merchants of Yang-chou: A study of commercial capitalism in eighteenth-century China'. *Harvard Journal of Asiatic Studies*, 130–168.
32. Ibid.
33. Ibid., p.135.
34. Ibid.
35. Kat Tai Tam (2009) *The Social Status and Thought of Merchants in Ming China, 1368–1644: A Foray into the Social Effects of the Commercialization of Ming China*. Downloaded from http://qspace.library.queensu.ca/jspui/bitstream/1974/5149/1/Tam_Kat_Tai_200908_MA.pdf
36. Ibid., p.67.
37. Ibid., p.70.
38. Ibid., p.62.
39. Finnane, A. (1993) 'Yangzhou: A Central Place in the Qing Empire', in Johnson, L. C. (ed.) *Cities of Jiangnan in Late Imperial China*. New York: State University of New York Press.

40. Cited in Ho (1954) pp.155–6.
41. Hsieh Chao-che cited in Ho (1954) p.143.

CHAPTER 6: THE CHINA INDUSTRY

1. Wang Shimao cited in Dillon, M. (1992) 'Transport and Marketing in the Development of the Jingdezhen Porcelain Industry during the Ming and Qing Dynasties.' *Journal of the Economic and Social History of the Orient/Journal de l'histoire economique et sociale de l'Orient*, 278–90, p.278.
2. Finlay, R. (2010) *The Pilgrim Art: Cultures of porcelain in world history.* University of California Press.
3. Medley, M. (2006) *The Chinese Potter: A practical history of Chinese ceramics.* London and New York: Phaidon Press.
4. Ibid.
5. Finlay (2010) and Medley (2006).
6. Finlay (2010).
7. Ibid.
8. Medley (2006).
9. Finlay (2010).
10. Dillon, M. (1976) *A history of the porcelain industry in Jingdezhen* (Doctoral dissertation, University of Leeds).
11. Ibid.
12. Cited in Gerritsen, A. (2009) Fragments of a global past: ceramics manufacture in Song-Yuan-Ming Jingdezhen. *Journal of the Economic and Social History of the Orient*, 52(1), 117–152.
13. Liu Dingzhi (1409–69) cited in Gerritsen (2009) p.132.
14. Dillon (1976).
15. Ibid.
16. Finlay (2010).
17. Gerritsen (2009).
18. Dillon (1976).
19. Ibid.
20. Ibid.
21. Ibid.
22. Ibid.

23. Raozhou Fuzhi cited in Dillon (1976) p.82.
24. Finlay (2010)
25. Finlay (2010) p.70.
26. Finlay (2010).
27. Ibid.
28. Dillon (1976).
29. D'Entrecolles (1906) The Letters of Père d'Entrecolles From William Burton's *Porcelain, It's Art and Manufacture*. London: B.T. Batsford. Downloaded from http://www.ceramicstoday.com/articles/entrecolles.htm
30. Finlay (2010).
31. Cited in Finlay (2010) p.65.
32. Polo Marco (1958) *The Travels*. London: Penguin, p.238.
33. Vashisth, A., and Kumar, A. (2013) 'Corporate espionage: The insider threat'. *Business Information Review*, 30(2), 83–90.
34. Findlay (2010).
35. D'Entrecolles (1906).
36. Ibid.
37. Finlay (2010).
38. D'Entrecolles (1906).
39. Ibid.
40. Finlay (2010).
41. D'Entrecolles (1906).
42. Ibid.
43. Dillon (1992).
44. Dillon (1976, 1992).
45. Dillon (1992) p.286.
46. Lan Pu cited in Dillon (1992) p.284.
47. Dillon (1976, 1992).
48. Cited in Gerritsen (2009) p.140.

CHAPTER 7: MERCHANT CULTURE IN THE LATE MING AND QING DYNASTIES

1. Cited in Brook, T. (2004) *Confusions of Pleasure: Commerce and culture in Ming China*. University of California Press, p.43.
2. Cited in Lufrano (1997) p.36.

3. Smith, J. F. H. (1998) 'Social hierarchy and merchant philanthropy as perceived in several Late-Ming and Early-Qing texts'. *Journal of the Economic and Social History of the Orient*, 41(3), 417–451.

4. Ibid.

5. Kai Tat Tam (2009) *The Social Status and Thought of Merchants in Ming China, 1368–1644: A Foray in Clarifying the Social Effects of the Commercialization of Ming China.*

6. Andrews, M. (2011) *Cultures of Commerce Compared: A comparative study of the ideal of the businessman in China and England, c. 1600-1800* (Doctoral dissertation, London School of Economics).

7. Lufrano (1997) pp.2–3.

8. Myers, R. H. and Wang, Y.-C., (2002) 'Economic developments, 1644–1800', in Peterson, W. J. (ed.), *The Cambridge history of China, volume 9, part 1: The Ch'ing empire to 1800.* Cambridge: Cambridge University Press, pp.563–645.

9. Chen, X. (1997) *Ming Qing shiqi shangye shu ji shangren shu zhi yanjiu* [*Research on business books and merchant books of the Ming and Qing periods*] Taibei.

10. Wang, Z. (1993) '*Ming Qing shiqi Huisheng shihui xingxiang de wenhua toushii*' ['A cultural perspective of the social image of Huizhou merchants in the Ming and Qing dynasties'], *Fudan Xuebao*, pp.80–4.

11. Cited in Andrews (2011) p.108.

12. Cited in Andrews (2011) p.106.

13. Andrews (2011).

14. Andrews (2011) p.108.

15. Santangelo (1993).

16. Golas, P. J. (1977) 'Early Qing guilds' in Skinner, G. W. *The City in Late Imperial China.* California: Stanford University Press, pp.555–80.

17. Ibid.

18. Golas (1977) p.579.

19. Du, X., Weng, J., Zeng, Q., and Pei, H. (2015) 'Culture, Marketization, and Owner-Manager Agency Costs: A Case of Merchant Guild Culture in China.' *Journal of Business Ethics*, 1–34.

20. What is Social capital? OECD Insights. Downloaded from http://www.oecd.org/insights/37966934.pdf on 9 June 2016

21. Golas (1977).
22. Ibid., p.571.
23. Gerritsen, A. (2009) 'Fragments of a global past: ceramics manufacture in Song-Yuan-Ming Jingdezhen.' *Journal of the Economic and Social History of the Orient*, 52(1), 117–152.
24. Lufrano (1997).
25. Ibid.
26. Ibid.
27. Chen (1997).
28. Lufrano (1997).
29. Ibid., p.10.
30. Ibid.
31. Ibid., p.47.
32. Cited in Andrews (2011) p.53.
33. Ibid., p.52.
34. Ibid.
35. Ibid., p.62.
36. Ibid., p.64.
37. Ibid., p.51.
38. Ibid., p.58.
39. Ibid.
40. Ibid.
41. Ibid., p.61.
42. Ibid.
43. Ibid., p.94.
44. Ibid., p.95.
45. Ibid., p.97.
46. Lufrano (1997) p.141.
47. Cited in Andrews (2011) p.94.
48. Ibid., p.95.
49. Ibid., p.94.
50. Ibid.
51. Cited in Andrews (2011) p.96.
52. Ibid.
53. Ibid., p.153.
54. Ibid.

55. Ibid., p.157.
56. Ibid.
57. Ibid., p.142.
58. Ibid., p.166.
59. Ibid., p.173.
60. Lufrano (1997) p.103.
61. Cited in Andrews (2011) p.123.
62. CIbid., pp.64–5.
63. Ibid., p.105.
64. Ibid., p.73.
65. Ibid.
66. Ibid., p.72.
67. Ibid., p.73.
68. Kai Tat Tam (2009).

CHAPTER 8: THE QING DYNASTY (1644–1911)

1. Du Halde, Pere P. J. B. cited in Dillon, M. (1992) 'Transport and Marketing in the Development of the Jingdezhen Porcelain Industry during the Ming and Qing Dynasties'. *Journal of the Economic and Social History of the Orient/Journal de l'histoire economique et sociale de l'Orient*, 278–290, p.283.
2. Marme, M. (1993) 'Heaven on earth: The rise of Suzhou 1127–1550'. In Cooke Johnson, L. (ed.) *Cities of Jiangnan in Late Imperial China*. Albany NY: State University of New York Press, pp.17–46.
3. Cooke Johnson, L. (1993) *Cities of Jiangnan in Late Imperial China*. New York: State University of New York Press.
4. Cited in Marme (1993) p.17.
5. Cooke Johnson (1993) p.ix.
6. Yu Gungwu cited in Santangelo, P. (1993) 'Urban society in late imperial Suzhou', in Cooke Johnson, L. (ed.) *Cities of Jiangnan in Late Imperial China*. Albany NY: State University of New York Press, p.85.
7. Zheng Ruoceng (1505–80) cited in Marme (1993) p.37.
8. Marme (1993).
9. Polo, M. (1817) *The Travels of Marco Polo* (translated by Marsden, W.). Published by author, p.505.

10. Rowe, W. T. (1993) 'Introduction: city and region in the lower Yangzi', in Cooke Johnson, L. (ed.), *Cities of Jiangnan in Late Imperial China*. Albany NY: State University of New York Press, pp.1–15.

11. Brook, T. (2004) *Confusions of Pleasure: Commerce and culture in Ming China*. University of California Press.

12. Ibid.

13. Ibid., p.198.

14. Brook (2004).

15. Santangelo (1993).

16. Ibid.

17. Ibid.

18. Ibid., p.91.

19. Ibid., pp.91–2.

20. Golas (1977).

21. Cited in Golas (1977) p.556.

22. Morck, R. and Yang, F. (2010) *The Shanxi Banks*, NBER Working Paper 15884 http://www.nber.org/papers/w15884

23. Ibid.

24. Shanxi Provincial Academy of Social Sciences (1992), *Shanxi piaohao shiliao* (山西票号史料) Taiyuan: Shanxi jingji chubanshe, pp.36–9.

25. Cheong, W. E. (1997) *The Hong Merchants of Canton: Chinese merchants in Sino-Western trade*. Richmond, Surrey: Curzon Press.

26. Ibid.

27. Ibid.

28. Van Dyke, P. A. (2011) *Merchants of Canton and Macao: Politics and strategies in eighteenth century trade*. Hong Kong and Kyoto: Hong Kong University Press and Kyoto University Press.

29. Cheong, W. E. (1979) *Mandarins and Merchants: Jardine Matheson & Co.: A China agency of the early nineteenth century*. London and Malmo: Curzon Press.

30. Van Dyke (2011) p.61.

31. Cheong (1979) p.18.

32. Ibid., p.29.

33. Van Dyke (2011).

34. Ibid.

35. Ibid.
36. Ibid.
37. Cheong (1997) p.93.
38. Cited in Van Dyke (2011) p.138.
39. Van Dyke (2011) p.140.
40. Van Dyke (2011).
41. Cheong (1997).
42. Cheong (1979).
43. Ibid., p.121.
44. Van Dyke (2011) p.10.
45. Cheong (1997).
46. Downs, J. M. (1968) 'American merchants and the China opium trade, 1800–1840'. *Business History Review*, 42(04), 418–442.
47. http://trove.nla.gov.au/newspaper/article/645302 *The Perth Gazette and Western Australian Journal*, Death of Howqua the Hong Merchant, 7 September 1844, p.3.
48. Ibid.
49. Le Pichon, A. (2010) 'Howqua and the *Howqua*: How a Chinese monopolist saved American free-traders from financial ruin'. *Journal of the Royal Asiatic Society Hong Kong Branch*, 50, 99–121.
50. Ibid., p.103.
51. Downs (1968).
52. Le Pichon (2010).

CHAPTER 9: OVERSEAS CHINESE IN SOUTH EAST ASIA

1. Department of Foreign Affairs and Trade (1995) *Overseas Chinese Business Networks in Asia*. Commonwealth of Australia, p.1.
2. Ibid. See also Hodder, R. (1996) *Merchant Princes of the East: Cultural delusions, economic success and the overseas Chinese in Southeast Asia*. New York: Wiley; and Lim, L. (1996). 'Southeast Asian Business Systems: The Dynamics of Diversity'. In Safarian, A. E. and Dobson, W. (eds), *East Asian Capitalism: Diversity and Dynamism*. Toronto: University of Toronto Press.
3. Wang Gungwu (1991) *China and the Chinese Overseas*. Singapore: Times Academic Press.

4. Borao, J. E. (1998) 'The massacre of 1603: Chinese Perception of the Spaniards in the Philippines'. *National Taiwan University: Itinerario*, 23(1)
5. Wang (1991).
6. Ibid., p.194.
7. Mahathir bin Mohammad (1970) *The Malay Dilemma*. Singapore Times Books International, pp.32–33.
8. Wang (1991).
9. Limlingan V. S. (1986) 'The Overseas Chinese in ASEAN: Business strategies and management practices'. Manila: Vita Development Corp.
10. Hicks, G. L., and Redding, S. G. (1982) 'Culture and corporate performance in the Philippines: The Chinese puzzle'. *Philippine Review of Economics*, 19(1 & 2).
11. Barton, C. A. (1983) 'Trust and credit: Some observations regarding business strategies of overseas Chinese traders in South Vietnam'. *The Chinese in Southeast Asia*, 1, 46–64.
12. Limlingan (1986).
13. Ibid., p.81.
14. See also Chu, T. C. and MacMurray, T. (1993) 'The Road Ahead for Asia's Leading Conglomerates'. *McKinsey Quarterly* 3, 117–126.
15. Limlingan (1986).
16. Palanca, E. H. (1995) *Chinese Business Families in the Philippines since the 1890s: Chinese Business Enterprise in Asia*. London: Routledge, pp.197–213.
17. *The Australian Financial Review*, 26 September 1995.
18. Sato, Y. (1993) 'The Salim group in Indonesia: the development and behaviour of the largest conglomerate in Southeast Asia'. *The Developing Economies*, 31(4), 408-441.
19. Doebele, J. (27 August 2004) 'Liem Sioe Liong'. *Forbes*. Retrieved 31 January 2010.
20. Department of Foreign Affairs and Trade (1995); Limlingan (1986); Sato, Y. (1993).
21. Oxfeld, E. (1993) *Blood, Sweat and Mahjong: Family and enterprise in an overseas Chinese community*. Ithaca, NY: Cornell University Press.
22. Bengal Past and Present 1909: 138–139 cited in Oxfeld (1993) p.73.
23. Cited in Oxfeld (1993) p.74.

24. Ibid., p.121.
25. Ibid., p.179.
26. Ibid.
27. Van Den Bulcke, D. and Zhang, H. Y. (1995) 'Chinese family-owned multinationals in the Philippines and the internationalisation process'. *Chinese Business Enterprise in Asia.* London: Routledge, 214–46.
28. Palanca (1995).
29. Van den Bulcke and Zhang (1995).
30. Ibid.
31. Department of Foreign Affairs and Trade (1995).
32. Van den Bulcke and Zhang (1995).
33. See also Redding, S. G. (1990) *The Spirit of Chinese Capitalism.* New York: De Gruyter.
34. Department of Foreign Affairs and Trade (1995).

CHAPTER 10: EVOLUTION OF THE ART

1. Redding, G. (1990) *The Spirit of Chinese Capitalism,* New York: de Gruyter. Redding, G. (1995) 'Overseas Chinese Networks: Understanding the enigma.' *Long Range Planning, 28*(1), 61–69; Department of Foreign Affairs and Trade (1995) *Overseas Chinese Business Networks in Asia,* Commonwealth of Australia, p.1
2. Redding (1995).
3. Department of Foreign Affairs and Trade (1995).
4. Dieleman, M., and Sachs, W. (2006) 'Oscillating between a relationship-based and a market-based model: The Salim Group.' *Asia Pacific Journal of Management, 23*(4), 521–536.
5. Department of Foreign Affairs and Trade (1995); see also Khanna, T. and Palepu, K. (1997) 'Why Focused Strategies May be Wrong for Emerging Markets'. *Harvard Business Review* July–August, 41–51.
6. Dieleman and Sachs (2006).
7. Hodder, R. (1996) *Merchant Princes of the East: Cultural delusions, economic success and the overseas Chinese in Southeast Asia.,* Sussex: Wiley.
8. Cited in Noss. J. B. (1980) *Man's Religions.,* New York: Macmillan, p.273.

9. Redding (1990, 1995).
10. Hodder (1996).
11. Department of Foreign Affairs and Trade (1995)
12. Wang Gungwu (1991) *China and the Chinese Overseas*. Singapore: Times Academic Press.
13. Redding (1995).
14. Downs, J. M. (1968) 'American Merchants and the China Opium trade 1800–1840.' *Business History Review*, 42(4): 418–442.
15. Ibid.
16. Cited in Ssu-yu Teng and John Fairbank, *China's Response to the West*, (Cambridge MA: Harvard University Press, 1954), reprinted in Mark A. Kishlansky, ed., *Sources of World History, Volume II.*, New York: HarperCollins College Publishers, 1995, pp. 266–9.
17. Le Pichon, A. (2006) *China Trade and Empire*. Oxford: Oxford University Press, p.40.
18. Hodder (1995).
19. Riskin, C. (1989) *China's Political Economy: The quest for development since 1949*. Oxford: Oxford University Press, p.13.
20. Cooke Johnson, L. (1993) 'Shanghai: An emerging Jiangnan port 1683–1840'. In Cooke Johnson, L. (ed.) *Cities of Jiangnan in Late Imperial China*. Albany NY: State University of New York Press, pp.151–81.
21. Wrigley, E. A. (2004) 'British population during the "long" eighteenth century, 1680–1840'. In Floud, R. and Johnson, P. (eds.) *The Cambridge Economic History of Modern Britain*, pp. 57–95. Available from: http://dx.doi.org/10.1017/CHOL9780521820363.004
22. Zimbalist, A., Sherman, H. J. and Brown, S. (1989) *Comparing Economic Systems*. Orlando FL: Harcourt Brace Jovanovich.
23. Zimbalist et al. (1989).
24. Naughton, B. (1993) 'Deng Xiaoping: The economist', *The China Quarterly*, 135, 491–515.
25. Naughton (1993).
26. Naughton (1993).
27. Xiaoping, D. (1987) *Fundamental Issues in Present-Day China* (Speeches, 1985–1986) Beijing: Foreign Languages Press, p.19.
28. Naughton (1993).

29. Lao Tzu (2000) *Tao Te Ching*, translated by David Hinton, Washington DC: Counterpoint, Verse 17.

30. Ying, X. and Clydesdale, G. (2010) 'Two Cultural Revolutions: Globalisation and Chairman Mao'. *International Journal of Chinese Culture and Management*, 3(1): 23–36.

31. Naughton (1993).

32. Dees, S. (1998) 'Foreign direct investment in China: determinants and effects'. *Economics of planning*, 31(2–3), 175–194.

33. Kanungo, A. K. (2007) 'Setting Up of Special Economic Zones in China Reforms and Policy Recommendations'. *Foreign Trade Review*, 42(2), 3–26.

34. Dees (1998).

35. Dees (1998), Kunungo (2007).

36. Kunungo (2007).

37. Erdener, C. and Shapiro, D. M. (2005) 'The internationalization of Chinese family enterprises and Dunning's eclectic MNE paradigm'. *Management and Organization Review*, 1(3), 411–436.

38. Yeung, H.W. C. (1999) 'The internationalization of ethnic Chinese business firms from Southeast Asia: Strategies, processes and competitive advantage.' *International Journal of Urban and Regional Research*, 23(1), 88–102, p.112.

39. Yeoh, C., and Wong, S. Y. (2010) 'Selective Intervention and Economic Re-Engineering: Lessons Form Singapore's Parks in Indonesia and India'. *Journal of Asian Business Studies*, 20(2), 13.

40. Dees (1998).

41. Kanungo (2007).

42. Ibid.

43. Ibid.

44. Keqiang, L. (2015) 'The economic blueprint'. *The World in 2016: The Economist*, London, p.52.

45. Quoted in Yeung, H. W. (2006) 'Change and continuity in Southeast Asian ethnic Chinese business'. *Asia Pacific Journal of Management*, 23(3), 229–254, p.242.

46. Yeung, H. W. C. (2000). 'The dynamics of Asian business systems in a globalizing era'. *Review of International Political Economy*, 7(3), 399–443.

47. Ibid.

48. Erdener and Shapiro (2005).

49. Dieleman and Sachs (2006) p.530.

50. Yeung (2006).

51. Peng, Au and Wang (2001a).

52. Yeung (2006).

53. Ibid.

54. Dieleman and Sachs (2006).

55. Yeung (2006).

56. Cited in Gelber, H. G. (2006) 'China as Victim: The Opium War that wasn't'. Harvard University Centre for European Studies, Working Paper 136.

57. Wang, J. (1999) *Entrepreneurship, Institutional Structures and Business Performance of the Overseas Chinese* (No. Discussion Paper No. 252).

Index